A DISCOURSE OF THE DAMNED ART OF WITCHCRAFT;

SO FARRE forth as it is revealed in the Scriptures, and manifest by true experience.

FRAMED AND DELIVERED BY

M. WILLIAM PERKINS,

Dedication

TO THE RIGHT HONOURABLE SIR EDWARD COOKE Knight, Lord cheife Justice of his Majesties Court of Common Pleas; Grace and Peace. Right Honourable: The word of God that onely Oracle of truth, hath pointed out the Enemie of mankinde, by his proper Characters, in sundry places. Our savior tearmes him, the Prince of this World; and a Murtherer from the beginning. Peter compares him to a roaring Lyon, that rangeth abroad in the earth, seeking whòm be may devoure. His attempts in regard of their qualitie, are called , subtile and deep devises; yea , plots exquisitely contrived, and so orderly framed, as it were in Methode. The meaning of the holy Ghost in these and such like attributes, is to expresse that measure of policie and power, which Satan hath reserved unto himselfe even in the state of his Apostacie, improoved by long experience, and instantly practised upon the sonnes of men, that he might set up in the world, a spirituall regiment of sinne, as a meane to encounter the kingdome of grace, and (if it were possible) to bring the same to ruine. To forbeare instances of open force made against God and his Church by other courses, for the compassing of his desires, how skilfully he works his owne advantage, by secret opposition, in the exercise of that cursed Art, which is the subject of the present Discourse, is a point not unworthy your Honourable consideration. The Power of this Prince of darkenes, beeing above the might of all sensible Creatures, and every way seconded by the greatnesse of his knowledge and experience, manifesteth it selfe herein, for the most part, by workes of wonder, transcendent in both sexes; sometime in matter of Divination, sometime by Inchantment, sometime by rare sleights and delusions; other whiles by hurting, by curing, by raising of Tempests, by speedy conveyance and transportation from place to place, and c. and all to purchase unto himselfe admiration, feare, and faith of the credulous world, which is usually carried away with affectation and applause of signes and wonders. His policie,

3

appeareth in a wise and exquisite manner of framing and conceiving both his practises and grounds; the one to procure credit and intertainement; the other that he may not faile of his purpose, but proceed upon certainties. Touching the manner of his practise. He stands resolved, that the world hath taken notice of him to be a lyar, and the father thereof: and therefore if he should offer to speake in his owne language, or informe an Art by rules of his owne devising; hee might happily incurred suspition of falsehood. Hereupon he composeth his courses , by way of counterfeit and imitation, not of the actions and dealings of men, but of the order of Gods owne proceeding with his Church; holding it a sure principle in policie, That actions will be much more effectual, when they bee framed after the best presidents, then when they are suited to the direction of meaner examples. To this purpose, as God hath made a Covenant with his Church, binding himselfe by promise to bee their God, and requiring of them the condition of faith and obedience; so doth Satan indent with his Subjects by mutuall confederacies, either solemnly or secretly; whereby they bind themselves on the one part to observe his Rules, and he on the other to accomplish their desires. Againe, God gives his Word, the Interpreter of his Will, and his Sacraments, the seales of his promises, to which beeing rightly administred and received, he hath tied his owne presence, and the worke of his grace in them that believe. Answerably to this, the Devil gives a word of direction to his instruments, and addeth unto it, Charmes, Figures, Characters, and other outward Ceremonies, at the use whereof he hath bound himselfe to be present, and to manifest his power in effecting the thing desired. Furthermore, God hath revealed his will to the Patriarchs, Prophets, and Apostles, by familiar conference, by dreames, by inspiration, by trances: In the same manner, Satan hath his Diviners, and Soothsayers, his Pythonisses, his Cassandraes, his Sybilles, to whome hee maketh knowne things to come, by familiar presence, by dreames, and c. To conclude, God had in the Olde Testament his Temple at

4

Jerusalem, yea his Oracle, from whence he spoke, and gave the answer unto Moses: So of ancient times, the Devil erected his Temple at Dodona, and Delphos, whence he gave his answers, for the satisfaction of the superstitious Heathen. Yea, and at this day, as the Ministers of God doe give resolution to the conscience, in matters doubtful and difficult: so the Ministers of Satan, under the name of wisemen, and wise-women, are at hand by his appointment, to resolve, direct, and helpe ignorant and unsettled persons, in cases of distraction, losse, or other outward calamities. Now the Grounds whereupon he buildeth his proceedings for certaintie, are cunningly gathered from the disposition of mans heart, by naturall corruption, and that in three speciall instances. First, he knowes that Man naturally out of the light of grace, hath but a meere soule, indued onely with some generall and confused notions; and as for matters of deeper apprehension touching God and heauenly things, there is a vaile of ignorance and blindnesse drawne ouer the eyes of his minde. Whereupon, though hee be apt to knowe and worship a God, and learne his will, yet for want of information by the word, he is prone to erre in the practise of his notion. Here Satan applyes himselfe to mans measure and at his owne will, drawes the minde into errour, by his delusions and impostures. This made the Samaritans in the Old Testament, and the superstitious Athenians in the Newe, to worship an unknowne God, that is, the 0 Devil. Hence it was, that the greatest Clerkes of Greece, 1 Thales, Plato, and the rest; for want of a better light, sought unto the Wizzards of Egypt, whom they called Prophets, men instructed by Satan in the grounds of Divination. And of this sort were Jannes and Jambres mentioned in the 2 Scriptures. Hence it was also that the ancient Heathen, having 3 no lawe and Testimonie from God, inquired at Soothsayers, and murmuring Inchanters; others betooke themselves in matters of doubt and difficultie, to the olde Oracles of 4 Jupiter Ammon in Libya, of 5 Jupiter Dodonæus at Dodona in Epirus; of 6 Apollo at Delphos, of 7 Jupiter Trophonius in B otia, and the rest; where the Devil

5

gave the answer, sometimes one way, and sometimes another. Secondly, Sathan by obseruation perciveth that man upon a 8 weake and ignorant minde, is prone superstitiously to dote upon the creatures, attributing some divine operation or vertue to them, without any ground of Gods word, or common understanding: and consequently disposed to worship God in some worke of man, or to joyne to the same worship the inventions of man, which he hath not commanded. Upon which ground he made the Heathen to dote upon their wisemen, to regard 9 Soothsayers, and them that wrought with Spirits. The Chaldean 0 Philosophers renowned for their superstitions and Magicall courses, to make the Heavens, fatalium Legum tabulam, ascribing that to the vertue of the Starres, which was knowne and done by Satanicall operation: The Magicians of Persia, to admit of corruptions in their ancient good learning, and to give themselves, upon the reading of the fabulous writings of the Chaldean Sorcerers, to the studie of unlawfull Arts invented by themselves, both before and after the times of Daniel the Prophet: Lastly, the ancient Romanes upon a superstitious dotage, never to undertake any businesse of waight, nisi auspicatô, unlesse they had lucky consent and warrant from the Colledges of their Augurers, erected by Romulus. Thirdly, there is a naturall Distemper in the minde of man, shewing it selfe in these particulars, That he cannot induce to stand in feare of imminent danger: That he swells in a high conceit of his owne deserts, especially when he is in lower estate then he would be: That he will not beare a wrong done without revenge: That he rests not satisfied with the measure of knowledge received, but affecteth the searching of things secret, and not revealed. When the minde is possessed with these troubled passions, with care to helpe it selfe; then comes the Devil, and ministreth occasion to use unlawfull meanes in the generall, and forceth the mind by continuall suggestion, to determine it selfe in particular upon his owne crafts. It was the case of Saul, and of Nebuchadnezzar. It caused many of the Heathen Philosophers, to goe from

Athens to Memphis, from Grecia to Syria, from men on earth to wicked spirits in hell, to get more illumination at the hands of the Prince of darkenesse. It moved sundry male-contented Priests of Rome, to aspire unto the chaire of Supremacie, by Diabolicall assistance; yea to exercise Magicall arts, when they were Popes: and thereby to manifest indeed, that they were not the true Successors of Simon Peter, but heyres of the vertues of Simon that Magus, who bewitched the people of Samaria, and professed to doe that by the great power of God, which he wrought by the aide and assistance of the Devil. If any doe thinke it strange, that Sathan should in this sort oppose himselfe to the kingdome of God, and maintaine his owne principlaitie, by such ungodly arts and exercises; They must knowe, that this and all other evils come to passe even by the will of God, who hath justly permitted the same: To punish the wicked for their horrible sinnes: as Saul for his wickednesse: To avenge himselfe upon Man for his ingratitude, who having the truth revealed unto him will not believe or obey it: To waken and rouze up the godly, who are sleeping in any great sinnes or infirmities: Lastly, to try and prove his people, whether they will cleave to him and his word, or seeke to Sathan and wicked spirits. Now from the consideration of the premisses, we conclude it a necessaire thing for the Church and people of God, to be acquainted with the dealing of Satan in this kinde, that knowing his subtile devises, they may learne to avoid them. For which purpose this Treatise was first framed, and now exhibited to your Lordship. The just commendation whereof, above others formerly divulged touching this Argument, appeareth herein, that it serveth to the full opening and declaration of Satans Methode in the ground and practises of Witchcraft. Wherein among many other remarkeable points, it may please you to take speciall notice of these particulars. I. That they doe grossely erre, who either in expresse tearmes deny that there be Witches, or in effect, and by consequent, avouching that there is no league between them and the Devil; or affirming they can doe no such miraculous workes as are

7

ascribed to them. The former issueth plainly out of the body of the Discourse. And for the latter; That there is a covenant between them, either explicite in manner and forme; or implicite by degrees of superstitious proceeding in the use of meanes insufficient in themselves; is plainly taught and confirmed in the same. That Witches may and doe worke wonders, is evidently prove: howbeit not by an omnipotent power, (as the gainsayer hath unlearnedly and improperly tearmed it) but by the assistance of Sathan their Prince, who is a powerfull spirit, but yet a Creature as well as they. And the wonders wrought by them, are not properly and simply miracles, but workes of wonder; because they exceed the ordinarie power and capacitie of men, especially such as are ignorant of Satans habilitie, and the hidden causes in nature, whereby things are brought to passe. II. That the Witch truely convicted, is to be punished with death, the highest degree of punishment; and that by the Law of Moses, the equitie where of is perpetuall. Yea, even the better Witch of the two in common reputation, because both are equally enemies to God, and true religion: and it is well knowne by true experience, that all professed Sorcerers, are guiltie of many most monstrous impieties. III. That the Miracles of the Popish Church at this day, are indeed either no miracles, or false and deceitfull workes. Touching corporall presence in the Sacrament, which they affirme to be by miracle: If it were true, then miracles were not yet ceased, but should still be as ordinary in the Church, as are the Sacraments. A point not onely confuted in the latter part of this Treatise, but also by testimony of purer Antiquitie. Augustine saith, That miracles were once necessary to make the world believe the Gospell: but hee that now seekes a signe that hee may believe, is a wonder, yea a monster in nature. Chrysostome concludeth upon the same grounds, That there is nowe in the Church, no necessitie of working Miracles; and calls him a false Prophet, that now takes in hand to worke them. Againe, if there be a miracle in the Sacrament, it is contrary to the nature of all those that were wrought, either by Moses and the Prophets, or by Christ, and his Apostles. For they were apparant to the eye, but this is insensible: and therefore neither of force to move admiration, nor to convince the minde of man, and make him to believe.

As for those which are pretended to be wrought by Saints, in that Church; if we make recourse to the Primitive times, wherein God gave the gift, to breede faith in the Gentiles; we shall finde that the power of producing such workes, was never actually inherent in the Apostles, but dispensed by them in the name of Christ. Neither was it in their libertie, to worke miracles when they would, but when it pleased God, upon speciall cause to call them thereunto. And if neither the power nor the will was in them, much lesse is it likely to be found in any of the Saints. And for their Reliques, of what name soever, so greatly magnified and resorted unto: we denie there is any such virtue in them. For they may not be thought to be more effectual then the hem of Christs garment, from which the power of healing the woman did not proceede, but from himselfe: or, then the Napkin of Paul, which did not cure the sicke, but the power of God onely, dispensed by the hands of Paul. Miracles therefore, avouched by them to be wrought at the Tombes and Statues of Saints, and by their Reliques and Monuments, are but meere Satanicall wonders, serving to maintaine Idolatrie and superstition: and are in truth, no better then the wonders of the Donatistes in S. Augustines time, aut figmenta menàacium hominum, aut portenta fallacium spirituum. IV. That the light of the Gospel purely preached, is a Soveraigne meane to discover and confound the power and pollicie of Sathan in Witchcraft and Sorcerie. The word of God preached, is the weapon of the Christians warfare, and is mightie through God to cast downe strong holds. At the dispensation of it by the Disciples of Christ, Sathan fell from heaven as lightening. After the ascension of Christ into Heaven, in the times of Claudius Cæsar, the Devil stirred up sundry persons, who in regard of the admirable works which they did, by the helpe of Magicke and Sorcerie, were accounted as Gods, and their Statues erected and worshiped with great recreance. Amongst the rest one Simon, called by a kind of eminencie Magus, practising his trade with successe, to the admiration of the multitude, was holden to be the great power of God: Whose dealing was first discovered by the light of the word, shining in the Ministerie of the Apostles, and himselfe convicted with such evidence of truth, to be an instrument of Sathan, that he was forced at length to flie out of Samaria into the Westerne parts, as Eusebius recordeth in his Ecclesiasticall Historie. By this, Christ the true Angell of the Covenant, locked and bound up Sathan for a 1000. yeares after his ascension, that he might not be so generally powerful in seducing the Gentiles, as he had been before his incarnation. But towards the expiration of those yeares, when corruption beganne to creepe into the Papacie: when the Bishops affected that Sea, and aspired unto it by Diabolicall Arts: when the Canons, Decrees, Sentences, Synodals, Decretalls, Clementines, Extravagant, with other Lawes and Constitutions, prevailed above the Scriptures: then began Satan againe to erect his kingdome, and these workes of iniquitie to be set abroach. These points, together with the whole worke ensuing, I humbly commend to your Honourable Patronage, that under your protection they may freely passe to the common viewe of the world. Wherein if I seeme over-bold, thus to presse upon your Lordship uknowne: my answer is at hand; That all by-respects set a part, I have been hereunto induced many wayes. First, upon a reverent opinion of those rare gifts of knowledge and pictie, wherewith God hath beautified your person, and thereby advanced you to high place, and estimation in this Common-wealth: Whereof those your grave and judicious speeches, even in the weightiest matters touching God and Cæsar, as also those many learned Law-writings, have given large testimonie. From which hath issued the greatnesse of your name, both in the present judgement of the world, and in future expectation. Next, our of a resolved perswasion of your honourable disposition, as in generall to the whole house of Leui, so particularly to those, whose labours have fruitfully flowed out of the Schools of the Prophets, amongst whom the Author of this Booke, in his time was none of the meanest. Lastly, by the consideration of the Argument, arising out of a Law Judiciall, agreeable to the calling and qualitie of a Judge. A Law penall in respect of the offence, and therefore suitable to his proceedings, whose office is to heare with favour, and to determine with equitie, to execute instice with moderation. A Law of the highest and greatest waight, immediately concerning God and his Honour, and therefore appertaining to him, that sits in the place of God, to maintaine his right, that hee may be with him in the cause and judgement.

By such Motives, I have encouraged my selfe, under assurance of your Lordships pardon, to present you with that, wherein you are most deservedly interested; further entreating of your favorable interpretation and acceptance, both of the qualitie of the Worke, and of the paines of the publisher. And thus heartily wishing to your Lordship increase of grace and honour, with a daily influence of blessing and direction from heaven, upon your grave consultations and employments, I humbly take my leave, and commend you to the grace of God, by whome doe rule all the Judges of the earth. Finchingfield. Octob. 26. 1608.

Your L. in all Christian dutie to be commanded,

TH. PICKERING.

A DISCOURSE OF WITCHCRAFT.

Thou shalt not suffer a Witch to live.

EXOD. 22. 18.

This Text containeth one of the Judiciall Lawes of Moses touching the punishment of Witchcraft: which argument I have chosen to entreat of, for these causes: First, because Witchcraft is a rife and common sinne in these our daies, and very many are intangled with it, beeing either practitioners thereof in their owne persons, or at the least, yeelding to seeke for helpe and counsell of such as practise it. Againe, there be sundry men who receive it for a truth, that Witchcraft is nothing else but a meere illusion, and Witches nothing but persons deluded by the devil: and this opinion takes place not onely with the ignorant, but is holden and *Denies the* maintained by such as are learned, who doe avouch it by *illusory* word and writing, that there be no Witches, but as I said *nature of* before. Upon these and such like considerations, I have been *witchcraft* moved to undertake the interpretation of this Judiciall Law, as a sufficient ground of the doctrine which shall be delivered. In handling whereof, two things are distinctly to be considered. The first what is a Witch. The second, what is her due and deserved punishment. And both these beeing opened and handled, the whole meaning of the law will the better appeare. For the first. To give the true description of a Witch, is a matter of great difficulties, because there be many differences and diversities of opinions touching this point: and therefore that we may properly, and truely define a Witch, we must first pause a while in opening the nature of Witchcraft, so farre forth as it is delivered in the bookes of the Olde and New Testament, and <u>may be gathered out of the true experience of learned and godly men</u>. Touching Witchcraft therefore I will consider three points. I. What Witchcraft is. II. What is the ground of the whole practise thereof. III. How many kinds and differences there be of it.

CHAP. I.

Of the Nature of Witchcraft.

To begin with the first: According to the true meaning of all the places of holy Scripture which treat of this point, it may bee thus described: Witchcraft is a wicked Art, serving for the working of wonders, by the assistance of the Devil, so farre forth as <u>God shall in justice permit</u>. Sect. I. I say it is an Art, *God allows* because it is commonly so called and esteemed amongst men, and there is reason why it should be thus tearmed. For as in all good and lawfull arts, the whole practise thereof is performed by certaine rules and precepts, and without them nothing can be done; <u>so witchcraft hath certain superstitious</u> *the rules &* <u>grounds and principles, whereupon it standeth, and by which</u> *precepts of* <u>alone the seats and practises thereof are commonly</u> *witchcraft* <u>performed</u>. If it be demaunded, what these rules be, and whence they had their beginning, considering that every Art hath reference to some author, by whom it was originally taught and delivered? I answer, that they are devised first by Satan, and by him revealed to wicked and ungodly persons of ancient time as occasion served: who receiving them from *witchcraft* him, became afterward in the just judgement of God, his *originated* instruments to report and convey them to others from hand *w/ Satan &* to hand. For manifestation whereof, it is to be considered, *is then handed* that God is not onely in generall a Soveraigne Lord and King *down by other* over all his creatures, whether in heaven or earth, none *witches* excepted, no not the devils themselves; but that he exerciseth also a speciall kingdome, partly of grace in the Church militant upon earth, and partly of glorie over the Saints and Angels, members of the Church triumphant in heaven. Now in like manner the Devil hath a kingdome called in Scripture the kingdome of darkens, whereof himselfe is the head and governour; for which cause he is tearmed the Prince of darkenesse, the God of this world, ruling and effectually working in the hearts of the children of disobedience. Againe, as God hath enacted Lawes, whereby his kingdome is governed, so hath the Devil his ordinances, whereby he keepeth his subjects in awe and obedience, which generally and for substance, are nothing else but transgressions of the very law of God. And amongst them all, the precepts of Witchcraft are the very cheife and most notorious. For by them especially he holds up his kingdome, and therefore more esteems the obedience of them, then of other. Neither doth he deliver them indifferently to every man, but to his owne subjects the wicked: and not to them all, but to some speciall and tried ones, whom he most be trusteth with his secrets, as beeing the fittest to serve turne, both in respect of their willingness to learne and practise, as also for their abilitie to become instruments of the mischief, which he intendeth to others. If it be here asked, whence the Devil did fetch and conceive his rules? I answer, out of the corruption and depravation of that great measure of knowledge he once had of God, and of all the duties of his service. For that being quite depraved by his fall, he turnes the same to the inventing and devising of what he is possible able, against God and his honour. Hereupon, well perceiving that God hath expressely commanded to renounce and abhor all practises of Witchcraft, he hath set broach this Art in the world, as a maine pillar of his kingdome, which notwithstanding is flatly and directly opposed, to one of the maine principall lawes of the kingdome of God, touching the service of himselfe in spirit and truth. Againe, the reason why he conveys these ungodly principles and practises from man to man is, because he findes in experience, that things are far more welcome and agreeable to the common nature of mankind, which are taught by man like unto themselves, then if the Devil should perfectually deliver the same, to each man in speciall. Hereupon, he takes the course at first to instruct some few onely, who being taught by him, are apt to convey that which they know to others. And hence in probabilities this devilish trade, had his first originall and continuance. Sect. II. In the second place, I call it a wicked Art, to distinguish it from all good and lawfull Arts, taught in schooles of learning, which as they are warrantable by the word of God, so are they no lesse profitable and necessary in the Church. Againe, to shew the nature and qualitie of it, that it is a most ungracious and wicked art, as appeareth by the Scriptures. For when Saul had broken the expresse commandement of God, in sparing Agag and the best things; Samuel tells him, that rebellion and disobedience is as the sin of Witchcraft, that is, a most horrible and grievous crime, like unto that wicked, capitall, and mother sinne, 1.Sam.15.23. Sect. III. Thirdly, I adde, tending to the working or producing of wonders; wherein is noted the proper ende of this art, whereby I put a further difference betweene it, and others that are godly and lawfull. Now if question bee moved, why man should desire by witchcraft to work wonders? I answer, the true and proper cause is this: The first temptation, whereby the Devil prevailed against our first parents, had inclosed within it many sinnes: for the eating of the forbidden fruite, was no small or single offence, but as some have taught, contained in it the breach of every Commandment of the Morall Law. Amongst the rest, Satan laboured to bring them to the sinne of discontentment, whereby they sought to become as Gods, that is, better then God had made them, not resting content with the condition of men. This sinne was then learned, and could never since be forgotten, but continually is derived from them to all their posterities, and now is become so common a corruption in the whole nature of flesh and blood, that there is scarce a man to bee found, who is not originally tainted therewith as he is a man. This corruption shews it selfe principally in two things, both which are the maine causes of the practises of Witchcraft. First, in mans outward estate; for he being naturally possessed with a love of himselfe, and an high conceit of his own deserving, when he lives in base and low estate, whether in regard of povertie, or want of honour and reputation, which he thinkes by right is due unto him; he then growes to some measure of griefe and sorrow within himselfe. Hereupon he is moved to yield himselfe to the Devil, to bee his vassal and scholler in this wicked art, supposing that by the working of some wonders, he may be able in time to relieve his povertie, to purchase to himselfe credit and countenance amongst men. It were easie to shewe the truth of this, by examples of some persons, who by these means have risen from nothing, to great places and preferment in the world. In stead of all, it appeareth in certain Popes of Rome, as Sylvester the second, Benedict the eight, Alexander the six, John 20. and the twenties one, and c. who for the attaining of the Popedome(as histories record) gave themselves to the Devil in the practise of Witchcraft, that by the working of wonders, they might rise from one step of honour to another, until they had seated themselves in the chair of Papacy. So great was their desire of eminence in the Church, that it caused them to dislike meaner conditions of life, and never to cease aspiring, though they incurred thereby the hazard of good conscience, and the losse of their soules. The second degree of discontentment, is in the minde and inward man; and that is curiositie, when a man resteth not satisfied with the measure of inward gifts received, as of knowledge, wit, understanding, memorie, and such like; but aspires to search out such things, as God would have kept secret: and hence he is moved to attempt the cursed Art of Magicke and Witchcraft, as a way to get further knowledge in matters secret and not revealed, that by working of wonders, he may purchase same in the world, and consequently rape more benefit by such unlawful courses, then in likelihood he could have done, by ordinarie and lawfull meanes. Sect. IV. Fourthly, it is affirmed in the description, that Witchcraft is practised by the assistance of the Devil, yet the more fully to distinguish it from all good, lawfull, and commendable Arts. For in them experience teacheth, that the Artsmaster is able by himselfe to practise his art, and to do things belonging thereunto, without the helpe of another. But in this it is other wise; for here the work is done by the helpe of another, namely, the Devil, who is confederate with the Witch. The power of effecting such strange workes, is not in the art, neither doth it flow from the skill of the Sorcerer, man or woman, but is derived wholly from Satan, and is brought into execution by vertue of mutuall confederacy, between him and the Magician. Now that this part of the description may be more clearly manifested, we are to proceed to a further point, to shew what kind of wonders they be which are ordinarily wrought by the ministerie and power of the devil. § 1. Wonders therefore be of two sorts; either true and plaine, or lying and deceitfull. A true wonder is a rate worke, done by the power of God simply, either above or against the power of nature, and it is properly called a miracle. The Scripture is plentifull in examples of this kind. Of this sort, was the deviding of the red sea, and making it dries land by a mightie east wind, that the children of Israel might passa through it, Exod. 14. 21. For though the East wind be naturally of great force to move the waters, and to drie the earth; yet to patt the sea asunder, and to make the waters to stand as walls on each side, and the bottom of the sea as a pavement, this is a worke simply above the naturall power of any wind, and therefore is a miracle. Againe, such were the wonder done by Moses and Aaron before Pharaoh in Egypt, one whereof, in stead of many, was the turning of Aarons rodde into a serpent, a worke truly miraculous. For it is above the power of naturall generation, that the substance of one creature should be really turned into the substance of another; as the substance of a rodde into the substance of a serpent. Of the like kind, were the standing of the Sunne in the firmament without moving in his course for a whole day, Josh. 10, 13. the going backe of the sunnein the firmament tenne degrees, 2. King. 20. 11. the preservation of the three men, Shadrach, Meshach, and Abednega, in the midst of the hot fierie furnace, Dan. 3.25. and of Daniel in the Lyons den, Dan. 6.22. the feeding of five thousand men, beside women and children, with five loaves and two fishes, Matth. 14. 20. 21. the curing of the eyes of the blind man with spittle and clay tempered together, INH.9.6, 7. and c. Now the effecting of a miracle in this kind, is a worke proper to God onely; and no creature, man, or Angell, can doe any thing either about or contraire to nature, but he

[margin, handwritten: wonders : miracles equated + as such only God can do them]

álone which is the Creator. For as God in the beginning made all things of nothing, so he hath reserved to himselfe, as a peculiar worke of his almighty power, to change or abolish the substance, property, motion, and use of any creature. The reason is, because he is the author and creator of nature, and therefore at his pleasure, is perfectly able to command, restraine, enlarge, or extend the power and strength thereof, without the helpe or assistance of the creature. Againe, the working of a miracle is a kind of creation; for therein a thing is made to be, which was not before. And this must needs be proper to God alone, by whose power, things that are, were once produced out of things that did not appeare. The conclusion therefore must needs be this, which David confesseth in the Psalme: God onely deth wondrous things, Psalm. 136.4 that is, workes simply wonderfull. But it is alleadged to the contrarie, that the Prophets in the olde Testament, and the Apostles in the new, did worke miracles. I answer, they did so, but how? not by their own power, but by the power of God, being onely his instruments, whom he used for some speciall purpose in those works; and such as did not themselves cause the miracle, but god in and by thé. The same doth Peter and John acknowledge, when they had restored the lame man to the perfect use of his limes, that by their power and godlinesse, they had not made the man to goe, Act. 3.12.

Again, it is objected, that our Savior Christ in his manhood wrought many miracles, as those before mentioned, and many more. Ans. Christ as he was man did something in the working of miracles, but not all. For in every miraculous worke there be two things; the worke it selfe, and the acting or dispensing of the worke: the worke it selfe, being by nature and substance miraculous, cósidering it was above or against the order of naturall causes, did not proceede from Christ as man, but from him as God; but the dispensation of the same, in this or that visible manner, to the view of men, was done and performed by his manhood. For example: The raising up of Lazarus out of the grave, having been dead four dayes, was a miracle, to the effecting whereof, both the Godhead and manhood of Christ concurred, by their several and distinct actions. The manhood onely uttered the voice, and bad Lazarus come forth, but it was the godhead of Christ that fetched his soule from heaven, and put it again into his bodie, yea which-gave life and power to Lazarus to heare the voice uttered, to rise and come forth, Joh. 11.43. In like manner, when he gave sight to the blind, Matth. 20. 34. he touched their eyes with the hands of his manhood, but the power of opening them, and making them to see, came from his Godhead, whereby he was able to doe all things. And in all other miraculous workes which he did, the miracle was always wrought by his divine power onely, the outward actions and circumstances that accompanied the same, proceeded from him as he was man. Now, if Christ as he is man, cannot worke a true miracle, then no meere creature can doe it, no not the Angels themselves, and consequently not Sathan, it beeing a meere supernaturall worke, performed onely by the omnipotent power of God. § 2. The second sort of wonders, are lying and deceitfull, which also are extraordinarie workes in regard of man, because they proceed not from the usual and ordinarie course of nature: and yet they be no miracles, because they are done by the vertue of nature, and not about or against nature simply, but above and against the ordinarie course thereof: and these are properly such wonders, as are done by Satan and his instruments: examples whereof we shall see afterwards. If any man in reason think it not likely that a creature should be able to worke extraordinarily by naturall meanes; he must remember, that though God hath reserved to himselfe alone the power of abolishing and changing nature, the order whereof he set and established in the creation, yet the alteration of the ordinarie course of nature, he hath put in the power of his strongest creatures, Angels, and Devils. That the Angels have received this power, and doe execute the same upon his command or permission, it is manifest by Scripture, and the proofe of it is not so

[margin: Christs miracles were performed by the conjunction of both his Divinity & his humanity. But ABSOLUTELY required his Divinity]

[margin: Lying & deceitful wonders not true miracles]

21

necessary in this place. But that Satan is able to doe extraordinarie works by the helpe of nature (which is the question in hand) it shall appeare, if wee consider in him these things. First, the devil is by nature a spirit, and therefore of great understanding, knowledge, and capacitie in all naturall things, of what sort, qualities, and condition soever, whether they be causes or effects, whether of a simple or mixt nature. By reason whereof he can search more deeply and narrowly into the grounds of things, then all corporall creatures that are cloathed with flesh and blood. Secondly, he is an ancient spirit, whose skill hath beene confirmed by experience of the course of nature, for the space almost of six thousand yeares. Hence hee hath attained to the knowledge of many secrets, and by long observation of the effects, is able to discerne and judge of hidden causes in nature, which man in likelihood cannot come unto by ordinarie meanes, for want of that opportunitie both of understanding and experience. Hereupon it is, that whereas in nature there bee some properties, causes, and effects, which man never imagined to be; others, that men did once knowe, but are now forgot; some which men knowe not, but might know; and thousands which can hardly, or at all be knowne; all these are most familiar unto him, because in themselves they be no wonders, but only mysteries and secrets, the vertue and effect whereof he hath sometime observed since his creation. Thirdly, he is a spirit of wonderful power, and might, able to shake the earth, and to confound the creatures inferiour unto him in nature and condition, if he were not restrained by the omnipotent power of God. And this power, as it was great by his creation, so it is not impaired by his fall, but rather increased and made more forcible by his irrecoverable malice he beareth to mankind, specially the seed of the woman. Fourthly, there is in the devil an admirable quickness, and a guilty, proceeding from his spirituall nature, whereby he can verie speedily and in a short space of time, convey himselfe and other creatures into places far distant one from another. By these foure helps, Satan is enabled to doe strange workes.

22

the Vast knowledge Satan possesses.

Fear of the Increased power of the Devil

Strange I say to man, whose knowledge since the fall is mingled with much ignorance, even in naturall things; whose experience is of short continuance, and much hindered by forgetfulness; whose agility by reason of his grosse nature, is nothing, if he had not the helpe of other creatures; whose power is but weakenesse and infirmitie in comparison of Satans. Yet if there be any further doubt, how Satan can by those helps worke wonders, we may be resolved of the truth thereof by considering three other things. First, that by reason of his great knowledge and skill in nature, he is able to apply creature, to creature, and the causes efficient to the matter, and thereby bring things to passe, that are in common conceit impossible. Secondly, he ~~bath~~ hath power to move them, not onely according to the ordinarie course, but with much more speed and celerity. Thirdly, as he can apply and move, so by his spirituall nature hee is able, if God permit, to convey himselfe into the substance of the creature, without any penetration of dimensions; and being in the creature, *Possession* although it be never so solide, he can worke therein not onely according to the principles of the nature thereof, but as far as the strength and ability of those principles will possibly reach and extend themselves. Thus it appeareth, that the devil can in generall worke wonders. § 3. Now more particularly, the Devils wonders are of two sorts. Illusions, or reall actions. An illusion is a worke of Sathan, whereby he deludeth or deceiveth man. And it is two-fold; either of the outward senses, or of the minde. An illusion of the outward senses, is *illusion as* a worke of the devil, whereby he makes a man to think that *deceite -* he heareth, seeth, feeleth, or toucheth such things as indeed *by manipulating* he doth not. This the devil can easily do diverse wayes, even *the eyes or* by the strength of nature. For example, by corrupting the *the air by* instruments of sense, as the humour of the eye, and c. or by *which* altering and changing the ayre, which is the meanes whereby *humans see.* we see; and such like. Experience teacheth us, that the devil is a skillfull practitioner in this kinde, though the meanes whereby he worketh such feats be unknown unto us. In this manner Paul affirmeth that the Galatians were deluded, whé he saith, O foolish Galatians, who hath bewitched you? Gal. 3. I. Where he seth a word, borrowed from the practise of Witches and sorcerers, who use to cast a miste (as it were) before the eyes, to dazzle them, and make things to appear unto them, which indeed they doe not see; and the ground of Pauls comparison, is that which he takes for a granted truth, that there be such delusions, whereby mens senses are and may be corrupted by satanical operation. Thus againe the devil by the Witch of Endor, deceived Saul in the appearance of Samuel, I. Sam. 28. making him believe that it had been Samuel indeed, whereas it was but a meere counterfeit of him, as shall appeare hereafter. Againe, the devil knowing the constitutions of men, and the particular diseases whereunto they are inclined, takes the vantage of some, and secondeth the nature of the disease by the concurrence of his own delusion, thereby corrupting the imagination, and working in the mind a strong perswasion, that they are become, that which in truth they are not. This is appar and #233;t in that disease, which is tearmed Lycáthropia, where some having their brains possessed and distempered with melancholy, have verily thought th and #233;selves to be wolves, and so have behaved théselves. And the histories of men in former ages, have recorded strange testimonies of some that have bin thus turned into wolves, lyons, dogs, birds, and other creatures, which could no be really in substance, but onely in appearance, and phantasie corrupted; and so these records are true. For God in his just judgment may suffer some men so to be bewitched by the devil, that to their conceit they may seeme to be like the bruite beasts, though in a deed they remaine the true men still. For it is a worke surmounting the devils power, to change the substance of any one creature, into the substance of an other. By this kind of delusion the church of Rome, in the times of blindnesse and ignorance, hath taken great advantage, and much encreased her riches and honour. For there be three points of the religion of that Church, to write, Purgatorie, Invocation of Saints, and honouring of Reliques, whereby she hath notably enriched

[margin note:] an interpretation of I Sam. 28 wherein Samuel's ghost is not raised. the necromancy here becomes mere deception against Saul.

[margin note:] Lycanthropy - another diabolical delusion - the unreality of metamorph- -osis

[margin note:] the Devil cannot truly transform people into animals but makes them believe they have been changed

24

her self: all which had their first foundation from these, and such like Satanicall impostures. For the onely way whereby they have brought the common sort to yield unto them, both for belief and practise, hath beene by deluding their outward senses, with false apparitions of ghosts and soules of men, walking and ranging abroad after their departure, and such like: whereby simple persons, ignorant of their fetches and delusions, have beene much affrighted, and caused through extremitie of feare and dread, to purchase their own peace and security, by many and great expenses. And indeed these were the strongest arguments that ever they had, and which most prevailed with the commó people, as is manifest in stories of all nations and ages, where such deceits have taken place, though oftentimes by the just judgement of God, they were taken in their craft, and their feats revealed. The second kind of illusion, is of the minde, whereby the devil deceives the minde, and makes a man thinke that of himselfe which is not true. Thus experience teacheth, that hee hath deluded mé both in former and later times, who have avouched and professed themselves to be Kings, or the sonnes of Kings. Yea some have holden themselves to be Christ, some to be Elias; some to be John the Baptist, and some extraordinarie Prophets. And the like conceits have entered into the minds of sundry witches, by the suggestion and perswasion of the devil. To whom, when they have wholly resigned their soules and bodies, they have been moved to believe things impossible touching théselves, as that they have indeed been changed into other creatures, as cats, birds, mise, and c. The inquisitions of Spaine and other countries wherein these and such like things are recorded, touching Witches really metamorphosed into such creatures, cannot bee true; considering that it is not in the power of the devil, thus to change substances into other substances. And those conversions recorded by them were onley Sathans illusions, wherewith the minds of Witches were possessed, and nothing else; which though they were extraordinaire (as the rest of this kinde are) yet they went not beyond the power of nature. The

[margin note: The Catholic Church implicit in these same kinds of deceits.]

[margin note: the distinction between illusions of the out ward senses and of the mind seems very thin.]

second sort of the devils wonders, are reall workes, that is, such as are indeede that which they seeme and appeare to bee. These, howsoever to men that knowe not the natures of things, not the secret and hidden causes thereof, they may seeme very strange and admirable, yet they are not true miracles, because they are not above and beyond the power of nature. If it be here alleged, that the devils works are not real and true actions, because the holy Ghost calleth them lying wonders, 2.Thess. 2.9. I answer, that they are called lying wonders, not in respect of the works themselves, for they were wonders truely done and effected; but in regard of the devils end and purpose in working them, which is to lie unto men, and by them to deceive. The truth of which point will appeare in the view of some particular examples. First, we reade in the Historie of Job, that Satan brought downe fire from heaven, which burnt up Jobs sheepe and servants, and caused a mighty winde to blow downe the house upon his childré, as they were feasting, to destroy them. Againe, he note the body of Job with botches and boyles. All these were true and real works, very strange and admirable, and yet no miracles, because they exceeded not the compasses of nature. For first, when hee cast downe the fire from heaven, he did not create the fire of nothing, for that is a worke proper to God alone, but applyed creature to creature and thereof produced such a matter as was fit to make fire of. If it be demanded, how he is able to doe this? we must remember, that his knowledge in naturall causes is great, and therefore he was not ignorant of the materiall cause of fire, which being throughly knowne and found out, Satan brought fire unto it, and so putting fire to the matter of fire, hee brought it down by his power and agility from heaven, upon the cattle and servants of Job. Againe, the wind which blew downe the house, where his sonnes and daughters were eating and drinking, was not created by the devil, but hee knowing well the matter whereof windes are generated naturally, added matter to matter, and thence came the wind; whereunto he joins himselfe, being a spirit of a swift and speedy nature, and

26

so makes it for his owne purpose, the more violent and forcible. Thirdly, he smote Jobs body with sore boiles, from the crown of his head to the sole of his foote. Now this may seeme strange that bee should have such power over mans body, as to cause such diseases to breed in it. Therefore we are further to understand, that his knowledge extendeth it selfe to the whole frame and disposition of mans body; whereby it comes to passe, that the causes of all diseases are well known unto him, and he is not ignorant how the humors in the body may be putrified, and what corrupt humors will breed such and such diseases, and by what meanes the aire it selfe may be infected; herupon preparing his matter, and applying cause to cause, he practiced upon the body of Job, and filled him with grievous sores. Another example of Satans reall workes is this. By reason of his great power and skill, he is able to appeare in the forme and shape of a má, and resemble any person or creature, and that not by deluding the senses, but by assuming to himselfe a true body. His power is not so large as to create a body, or bring againe a soule into a body, yet by his dexterity and skill in natural causes he can work wonderfully. For he is able having gathered fit matter to joyne member to member, and to make a true body, either after the likeness of man, or some other creature; and having so done, to enter into it, to move and stir it up and down, and therein visibly and sensibly to appeare unto má: which though it is a stráge work, and besids the ordinarie course of nature, yet it is not simply above the power thereof. For a third instance. The devil is able to utter a voice in plaine words and speech, answerable to mans understanding in any language. Not that he can take upon himselfe, being a spirit, an immediate power to speak or frame a voice of nothing without meanes, but knowing the naturall and proper causes and meanes by which men doe speak, by them he frames in himselfe the voice of a man, and plainely utters the same in a knowne language. In this manner he abused the tongue and mouth of the serpent, when in plaine words he tempted Eve to eate the forbidden fruit.

Now it is to be remembered here, that when the devil speakes in a creature, it must be such a creature, as hath the instruments of speech, or such whereby speech may be framed and uttered, not otherwise: for it was never heard that he spoke in a stock or stone, or any created entity, that had not the meanes and power of uttering a voice, at least in some sort; it being a worke peculiar to the Creator, to give power of utterance where it is not by creation. Againe, when he frameth a voice in a creature, he doth it not by giving an immediate power to speak, for that he cannot do, and the creature abused by him, remaineth in that regard, as it was before. But it being naturally fitted and disposed to utter a voice, though not perfectly to speak as a man, he furthereth and helpeth nature in it, and addeth to the facultie thereof a present use of words, by ordering and ruling the instruments, to his intended purposes. And to conclude this point, looks what strange works and wonders may be true effected by the power of nature, (though they be not ordinarily brought to passe in the course of nature) those the devil can do, and so far forth as the power of nature will permit, he is able to work true wonders, though for a false and evil end. Here a question is moved by some, whether the devil can change one creature into another, as a man or a woman into a beast? for some not-withstanding the doctrine already taught, are of opinion, that he can turn the bodies of Witches into other creatures, as hares, cartes, and such like. Ans. The transmutation of the substance of one creature into another, as of a man into a beast of what kind soever, is a work simply above the power of nature, and therefore cannot be done by the devil, or any creature. For it is the proper worke of God alone, as I have said, to create, to change, or aboid nature. It is objected, that such changes have been made. For Lots wife was turned into a pillar of salt, Gen.19.26. Ans. It is true, but that was done by the mighty power of God, neither can it be proofed, that any creature, angel, or other, was ever able to doe the like. But it is further said, that king Nebuchadnezzar was turned into a beast, and did eate grasse with the beasts of the field,

Dan.4.30. Answ. There is no such matter: his substance was not changed, so as his bodie became the bodie of a beast indeed, but his conditions onely were altered by the judgement of God upon his mind, whereby he was so farre forth bereaved of humane sense and understanding. Againe, for his behaviour and kind of life, he became altogether brutish for the time, and excepting onely his outward forme and shape, no part of humanity could appeare in him: but that he retained his humane bodie still, it is evident by his owne words, vers.31. when he saith, And mine understanding was restored to mee: which argueth plainly that the hand of God was upon him in some kind of madness and furie, and therefore that there was not a change of his bodie and substance, but a strange and fearefull alteration in his minde and outward behaviour. And though such a transmutatió should be granted, yet it makes nothing for the purpose, considering it was the worke of God onely, and not of the devil. And thus we see what kind of wonders the Devil can bring to passe. The meditation of which point may teach us two things. First, that the working of wonders is not a thing that will commend man unto God: for the devil himselfe a wicked spirit, can worke them: and many shall alleadge this in the day of indgement, that they have by the name of God cast out devils, and done many great workes; to whom not withstanding the Lord will say, I never knewe you: depart from me yee workers of iniquitie, Matth.7.22,23. It behooueth us rather to get unto our selves the precious gifts of faith, repentance, and the feare of God; yea to goe before others in a godly life and upright conversation, then to excell in effecting of strange workes. When the seaventie Disciples came to our Savior Christ with joy, and told him, that even the devils were subdued unto them through his name, Luk.10.17. he counsels them not to rejoyce in this, that wicked spirits were subdued unto them, but rather, because their names were written in heaven, vers.20. Indeed, to be able to worke a wonder, is an excellent gift of God, and may minister matter of rejoycing, who it proceedeth from God:

but seeing the devil received this power by the gift of creation, our speciall joy must not be therein, but rather in this, that we are the adopted sonnes of God, in which privilege the devil hath no part with us. And therefore the Apostle, 1. Cor.,13. making a comparison of the gifts of the spirit, as of speaking divers tógues, of prophecying, and working miracles, with love: in the ende, wisheth men to labour for the best gifts, which are faith, hope, and love, because by these wee are made partakers of Christ, on whom we ought to set our hearts, and in whom we are commanded alwaies to rejoyce, Phil.4.4. Secondly, we learne from hence, not to believe or receive a doctrine now or at any time, because it is confirmed by wonders. For the devil himselfe is able to confirme his errours and Idolatrous services, by strange and extraordinaire signes, by which usually hee laboureth to avouch and verefie the grossest points of falsehood in matter of religion. On the contrarie, we must not reject or contemn a doctrine, because it is not thus confirmed. This was a main fault in the Jewes, who would not receive the word preached by Christ, unlesse hee shewed them a signe from heaven. Indeed in the primitive Church it pleased God to confirme that doctrine which the Apostles taught, by great signes and miracles, but now that gift is ceased, and the Church hath no warrant to expect any further evidence of the religion it professeth and enjoyeth by arguments of that kind; yea rather it hath cause to suspect a doctrine taught for the wonders sake, whereby men labour to auouch it. Sect. V. The last clause in the description, is this; so far forth as God in instice suffereth: which I adde, for two causes. First, to shew that God, for just causes, permitteth the Arts of Magicke and Witchcraft, and the practises there of. Now this he doth in his providence, either for the trial of his children, or for the punishment of the wicked. First, therefore God permits these wicked arts in the Church, to prove whether his children will steadfastly believe in him, and seek unto his word, or cleave unto the Devil, by seeking to his wicked instruments. This Moses plainly forewarned the church of God in his time; Deu.13.v.1. If there arise among you a Prophet, or a dreamer of dreames, and give thee a signe or wonder, v. 2. and the signe and wonder which hee hath told thee, come to passe: saying, Let us go after other gods, which thou hast not knowne, and serve them, vcr. 3. thou shalt not hearken to the words of that prophet.

Againe, God suffereth them for the punishment of unbelievers and wicked men: for oftentimes God punisheth one sinne by another, as the antecedent sins by the consequent. This Paul plainely sheweth (speaking of the daies of Antichrist) that because men received not the love of the truth, therefore God would send upon them strong illusions, that they should believe lies. And we may resolve out selves, that for this very cause, God suffereth the practises of Witchcraft, to be so rife in these our dayes, to punish the in gratitude of men, who have the truth revealed unto them, and yet will not believe and obey the same, but tread it under their feete, that all they might be condemned which believed not the truth, but took pleasure in unrighteousness. Secondly, this last clause is added, to shew that in the practises of sorcerie and Witchcraft, the Devil can doe so much onely as God permits him, and no more. Doubtless, his malice reacheth further, and consequently his will and desire; but God hath restrained his power, in the execution of his malicious purposes, whereupon he cannot goe a whit further, then God gives him leave and liberties to goe. The Magicians of Egypt did some wonders, in shew like unto the miracles wrought by Moses and Aaron, and that for a time, by changing a rodded into a serpent, and water into blood, and by bringing frogs through the flight and power of the Devil; but when it pleased God to determine their practises, and give them no further libertie, they could not doe that, which in likelihood was the meanest of all the rest, the turning of the dust of the land into lice; and themselves gave the true reason thereof, saying, That this was the finger of God, Exod. 8. 19. When the devil went out and became a false spirit in the mouth of all Ahabs Prophers, to entise him to goe to fall at Ramoth Gilead, he went not of his owne will, but by the authoritie of God, who commanded him to goe to entise Ahab, and suffered him to prevail, 1. King. 22. 22. and the act was not the act of Sathan, but of God, whose instrument he was; and therefore the holy Ghost said by Micaiah, The Lord hath put a lying spirit in the mouth of all these thy Prophets, and the Lord hath appointed evil against thee, v. 23. Hence also it was, that the devils, being cast out of the man that had an unclean spirit, asked leave of Christ to enter into the heard of swine, and could not enter in till he had permitted them; Mark. 5. 12, 13. And we reade oftentimes in the Gospel, that our Savior cast out many devils by his word onely, thereby shewing that he was absolute Lord over them, and that without his permission, they could doe nothing. And thus much touching: he general nature of this Arte.

CHAP. II.

The Ground of Witch- craft, and of all the practises thereof.

THe Ground of all the practises of Witchcraft, is a league or covenant made betweene the Witch and the Devil: wherein they doe mutually bind themselves each to other. If any shall thinke it strange, that man or woman should enter league with Satan, their utter enemie; they are to know it for a most evident and certaine truth, that may not be called into question. And yet to cleare the judgement of any one in this point, I will set downe some reasons in way of proofe. First, the holy Scripture doth intimate so much unto us in the 58. Psal.v. 5. where, howsoever the common translation runneth in other tearmes, yet the words are properly to be read thus: which heateth not the voyce of the mutterer joyning societies cunningly. And in them the Psalmist layeth downe two points. First, the effect or worke of a charme, muttered by the Inchanter; hamely that it is able to stay the Adder from stinging those which shall lay hold on him, or touch him. Secondly, the maine foundation of the charme; societies or confederacies cunningly made, not betweene man and man, but (as the words import) betweene the Inchanter and the Devil. The like we reade, Deut, 18, 11. where the Lord chargeth his people when they come into the land of Canaan, that amongst other abominations of the heathen, they should beware least any were found amongst them, that joyned society, that is, entered into league and compact with wicked spirits. A second reason may be this: it is the practise of the devil to offer to make a bargains and covenant with man. Thus he dealt with our Savior Christ in the third temptation, wherewith he assaulted him, promising to give unto him all the kingdomes of the earth, and the glory of them, (which he shewed him in a vision) if Christ for his part would fall downe and worship him. The offer was passed on the behalfe of Sathan, and now to make a perfect compact betweene them, there was nothing wanting but the free consent of our

Savior unto the condition propounded. Whereby it is manifest, that the devil makes many covenants in the world, because he findeth men and women in the most places, fitted for his turne in this kind, who will not let to worship him for a farre lesse matter then a king dome. And it is not to be doubted, that thousáds in the world, had they beene offered so faire as Christ was, would have bin as willing to have yielded upon such conditiós, as the devil to have offered. Thirdly, the common confession of all Witches and Sorcerers, both before and since the comming of Christ, doth yet more fully confirme the same. For they have confessed with one consent, that the very ground-work of all their practises in this wicked art, is their league with the devil. And hence it appeareth, how and whereupon it is, that Sorcerers and Witches can bring to passe strange things by the helpe of Satan, which other men ordinarily cánot do; namely, because they have entered a league with him, whereby he hath bound himselfe to them, for the effecting of rare and extraordinarie workes, which others not joyned with him in the like confederacie, are not able either by this helpe, or any power or pollicie of their own to bring to passe. Hereupon it was, that the witch of Endor shewed unto Saul the appearance of Samuel, which neither Saul himselfe, nor any in al his court could doe. There was no great vertue in the matter or frame of her words, for she was ignorant and had no learning. By power she could not effect it, being a weake woman; neither was it like that she had more cunning and pollicie then any of the learned Jewes in those times had for such purposes. The maine reason was her league made with Sathan, by vertue whereof she commanded him to appeare in the likenesse of Samuel, which neither Saul, nor any of his company could do, by vertue of such covenant, which they had not made. The end why the Devil seeketh to make a league with men, may be this; It is a point of his pollicie, not to be ready at every mans command to doe for him what he would, except he be sure of his reward; and no other meanes will serve his turne for taking assurance hereof, but this covenant. And why so?

34

that hereby he may testify both his hatred of God, and his malice against man. For since the time that he was cast downe from heaven, he hath hated God and his kingdome, and greatly maligned the happy estate of man, especially since the covenant of grace made with our first parents in Paradise. For he thought to have brought upon them by their fall, eternal and final confusion; but perceiving the contrary by vertue of the covenant of grace, then manifested, and seeing man by it to be in a better and surer estate then before, he much more maligned his estate, and bears the ranker hatred unto God for that his mercy bestowed upon him. Now that hee might shewe forth his hatred and malice, he takes upon him to imitate God, and to counterfeit his dealings with his Church. As God therefore hath made a Covenant with his people, so Satan joynes in league with the world, labouring to bind some men unto him, that so if it were possible, he might draw them from the covenant of God, and disgrace the same. Againe, as God hath his word and Sacraments, the seales of his covenant unto believers; so the devil hath his words and certaine out ward signes to ratified the same to his instruments, as namely, his figures, characters, gestures, and other Satanicall ceremonies, for the confirmation of the truth of his league unto them. Yea further, as God in his covenant, requires saith of us to the believing of his promises: so the devil in his compact, requires faith of his vassalls, to put their affiance in him, and rely on him for the doing of whatsoever he bindes himselfe to doe. Lastly, as God heares them that call upon him according to his will, so is Satan ready at hand upon the premisses, endeavoring to the utmost of his power (whe God permits him) to bring to passe whatsoever he hath promised. And so much of the league in generall. More particularly, the league between the Devil and a Witch, is twofold: either expressed and open, or secret and close. The expresse and manifest compact is so tearmed, because it is made by solemne words on both parties. And it is not so expressely set downe in Scriptures, as in the writings of learned men, which have recorded the confessions of

Witches: and they expresse it in this manner. First, the Witch for his part, as a slave of the devil, bindes himselfe unto him by solemn vow and promise to renounce the true God, his holy word, the covenant he made in Baptisms, and his redemption by Christ; and withall to believe in the Devil, to expect and receive aide and helpe from him, and at the ende of his life, to give him either body, or soule, or both: and for the ratifying hereof, he gives to the devil for the present, either his owne hand writing, or some part of his blood, as a pledge and earnest penny to bind the bargaine. The devil on the other side, for his part promiseth to be ready at his vassals command, to appeare at any time in the likeness of any creature, to consult with him, to aide and helpe him in any thing he shall take in hand, for the procuring of pleasures, honour, wealth, or prefer ment, to goe for him, to carry him whether he will; in a word, to doe for him, whatsoever hee shall command. Many sufficient testimonies might be alleadged for the proofe hereof, but it is so manifest in daily experience, that it cannot well be called into question. But yet if it seeme strange unto any, that there should be such persons in the world, that make such fearefull covenants with the devil, let them consider but this one thing, and it will put them out of doubt. The nature of man is exceeding impatient in crosses, and outward afflictions are so tedious unto mortal mindes, and presse them with such a measure of griefe, that some could be contented with all their hearts to be out of the world, if thereby they might be released of such extremity; and hereupon they care not what means they use, what conditions they undertake to ease and helpe themselves. The denial finding men in these perplexities, is readie to take his advantage, and therefore perceiving them now fitted for his purpose to work upon; he insinuates, and offers himselfe to procure them ease and deliverance, if they will use such means, as he shall prescribe for that purpose: and to a naturall man there is no greater mean then this to make him joyne societie with the devil. Hee therefore, without any further doubting or deliberation, condescends to Satan, so as he may be eased and relieved in these miseries. Again, we are to consider, that in these cases the devil getteth the greater hold of man, and moves him to yield unto his suggestions the rather, because that which he promiseth to doe for him is present and at his command, and therefore certaine; whereas the thing to be perforḿéd on the behalfe of the party himselfe, as the giving of body and souls, and c. is to come sundry years after, and therefore in regard of the particular time uncertain. Now the natural man not regarding his future and final estate, preferres the present commodities before the losse and punishment that is to come a far off, and thereby is perswaded to yield himselfe unto Satan. And by these and such like antecedents are many brought to make open league with the devil. The secret and close league betweene the Witch and Satan is that, wherein they mutually give consent each to other, but yet without a sworn covenant conceived in expresse words and conference. Of this there be two degrees. First, when a man useth superstitious formes of prayer, wherein hee expressely requireth the helpe of the devil, without any mention of solemne words or covenant going before. That this is a kinde of compact it is plaine, because herein there is a mutuall under-hand consent, betweene the party and the devil, though it be not manifest. For when a man is content to use superstitious formes of invocation, for help in time of neede; by the very using of them, his heart consenteth to Sathan, and he would gladly have the thing effected. When therefore the devil hath notice of them, and indeavoureth to effect the thing prayed for, therein also he gives cósent; so as though there be no expresse words of cópact outwardly framed on both parts, yet the concurrence of a mutuall consent for the bringing to passe of the same things, makes the covenant authenticall. For according to the received rules of equity and reason; mutuall consent of partie with party, is sufficient to make a bargain, though there be no solemn course or forme of words to manifest the same to others. The second degree is, when a man useth superstitious meanes to bring any thing to passe, which in his owne

[margin annotations: a covenant between the Witch + Satan w/out a formal Pact.]

[margin annotations: the use of superstitions prayers pleading aid from the Devil.]

[margin annotations: resort to human laws to explain a covenant.]

37

knowledge, hath no such vertue in themselves to effect it, without the especiall operation of the devil. Superstitious meanes, I call all those, which neither by order of creation, nor by the special appointment and blessing of God since, have any vertue in them, to bring to passe that thing for which they are used. For example; A charm, cósisting of set words and syllables, both rude, barbarous, and unknowne, used for the curing of some disease or paine, is a superstitious meanes, because it hath no vertue in it selfe to cure, either by the gift of God in the creation, or by any special appointment afterward in his word or otherwise. And therefore when this meane is used by man, which he knoweth hath no such vertue in it, for the effecting of that worke for which it was used, there is a secret league made with the Devil. Yet here I adde this clause, in his owne knowledge, to put a difference betweene men, which use superstitious meanes, to bring some things to passe: For some there be which when they use them, know they are meerely superstitious, yea weake and impotent, having no vertue in themselves for the purpose whereto they are used; as the repeating of certaine formes of words; the using of signes, characters, and figures, which in effect are meere charmes, no whit effectuall in themselves, but so farre forth as they serve for watchwords unto Satan, without whose aide nothing is done by them. A plaine argument that the user hereof hath in his heart secretly indented with Satan, for the accomplishment of his intended workes. A second sort there is, which useth them for some speciall ende, beeing perswaded that there is vertue in the means these to bring the thing to passe, and yet not knowing that either they be superstitious, or have their efficacy by the power and worke of the devil. Such persons have made as yet no league with Satan, but they are in the high way thereunto. And this course is a fit preparatió to cause them to joyne with him in covenant. I shew it by an example. A man is fallen into some extremity, and finds himselfe bewitched; his paine is great, and he desires with all his heart to bee cured and delivered: Hereupon he sendeth for the suspected Witch;

38

being come, he offers to scratch him or her, thinking by this meanes to bee cured of the Witchcraft. His reason is no other, then a strong perswasion, that there is simply vertue in his scratching to cure him, and discover the Witch, not once suspecting that the helpe commeth by the power of the Devil, but from the action it selfe. This doing, he may be healed: but the truth is, he sinneth and breakes Gods commandant. For the using of these meanes is plaine Witchcraft, as afterward we shall see. And yet for all this, the party cannot be said in present to have made a league with Satan, because he thought, that though he yielded to the use of superstitious meanes for his curing, yet there had been in the said meanes a vertue of healing, without any helpe or worke of the devil.

CHAP. III.

Of the kindes of Witchcraft, and first of Divination.

Witchcraft is of two sorts; Divining, or Working. For the whole nature of this art, consisteth either in matter of Divination and conjecture, or in matter of practise. And in both these it is to be remembered, that nothing can be effected, unless the party have made a league with the Devil, expresse or secret, or at the least, a preparation thereunto, by a false and erroneous opinion of the meanes. Sect. I. Divination is a part of Witchcraft, whereby men reveal strange things either past, present, or to come, by the assistance of the Devil. If it be here demanded, how the devil being a creature, should be able to manifest and bring to light things past, or to foretell things to come: I answer, first generally, that Satan in this particular work, transformed himselfe into an Angell of light, and takes upon him the exercise of these things in an ambitious (though false) imitation of divine revelations and predictions, made and used by God in the times of the Prophets and Apostles. And thus he doth (as much as in him lieth) to obscure the glory of God, and to make himselfe great in the opinion of ignorant and unbelieving persons. Again, though Satan be but a creature, yet there be sundry wayes whereby he is able to divine. First, by the Scriptures of the Old and New Testament, wherein are set downe sundry prophecies concerning things to come. In the Old Testament are recorded many prophecies concerning the state of Gods church, from the first age of the world, till the comming of Christ. In the new Testament like wise are recorded others, touching the selfe same thing, fró the cóming of Christ in the latter dayes, to the ende of the world. Now the devil being acquainted with the historie of the Bible, and having attained unto a greater light of knowledge in the prophecies therein contained, then any man hath; by stealing divinations out of them, he is able to tell of many strange things, that may in

Magic onely works by virtue of an expres or impleet pact or to set one on the road toward a pact.

the Devil gives false divinations to obscure + undermine the glory of God.

40

time fall out in the world, and answerably may shew them ere they come to passe. For example; Alexander the great before hee made warre with Darius King of Persia, consulted with the Oracle, that is, with the Devil, touching the event and issue of his enterprise. The Oracle answered him thus; Alexander shall be a conqueror; upon the prediction of the Oracle, Alexander wages warre with Darius, and invades Asia, and having conquered him, translated the Empire from Persia to Greece, according as the Oracle had said. Now if question be made, how the devil knew the event of this warre, and consequently made it knowne to Alexander? The answer is, by the helpe of a prophecie in the Olde Testament; for this thing was particularly set down before hand by the Prophet Daniel, Dan. 11.3. where he saith; That a mighty King shall stand up, and shall rule with great dominion, and doe according to his pleasure: and this was Alexander the great. Satan therefore knowing the secret meaning of the Angels words unto Daniel, framed out of them a true and direct answer, whereas he was not able of himselfe to define certainly of the event of things to come in particular. The second meanes, whereby the Devil is furnished for this purpose, is his own exquisite knowledge of all naturall things; as of the influences of the stars, the constitutions of men, and other creatures, the kinds, virtues, and operations of plants, rootes, hearbs, stones, and c. which knowledge of his, goeth many degrees bey and the skill of all men, yea even of those that are most excellent in this kind, as Philosophers, and Physicians. No marvel therefore, though out of his experience in these and such like, he is able a forehand to give a likely gesse at the issues and events of things, which are to him so manifestly apparent in their causes. A third helpe and furtherance in this point, is his presence in the most places; for some devils are present at all assemblies and meetings, and thereby are acquainted with the consultations and conferences both of Princes and people; whereby knowing the drift and purpose of mens mindes, when the same is manifested in their speeches and deliberations, they are the

[handwritten margin note: Daniel prophesied about Alexander the Great? Really?]

41

fitter to foretell many things, which men ordinarily cannot doe. And hence it is apparent, how Witches may know what is done in other countries, and whether one nation, intends warre against another, namely, by Satans suggestion, who was present at the consultation, and so knew it, and revealed it unto them. But how then comes it to passe, that the consultations and actions of Gods Church and children, are not disclosed to their enemies? even by the unspeakable mercie and goo darkness of God, who though for speciall causes sometimes, he suffers Satan by this meanes to bring things to light, yet he hath restrained this his liberty, and subiected it unto his owne will, so as he keeps him out of such meetings, or compels him to conceale; whereas otherwise his malice is so great, that not a word could be spoken, but it should be carried abroad to the hurt and disturbance both of churches and common-wealths. The fourth way, is by putting into mens mindes wicked purposes and counsels; for after the league once made, he laboureth with them by suggestions, and where God gives him leave, he never ceases perswading, till he hath brought his enterprise to passe. Having therefore first brought into the mind of man, a resolution to doe some evil, he goes and reveal it to the Witch, and by force of perswasion upon the party tempted, he frames the action intended to the time foretold, and so finally deludes the Witch his owne instrument, foretelling nothing, but what himselfe hath compassed and set about. The fist helpe, is the agilitie of Satans nature whereby he is able speedily to convey himselfe from place to place, yea to passe through the whole world in a short time For god hath made him by nature a spirit, who by the gift of his creation, hath attained the benefit of swiftness, not onely in dispatching his affaires, but also in the carriage of his person, with great expedition for the present accomplishment of his own desires. Lastly, God doth often use Sathan as his instrument, for the effecting of his intended workes, and the executing of his judgements upon men; and in these cases manifesteth unto him, the place where; the time when, and

42

the manner how such a thing should be done. <u>Now all such things as God will have effected by the devil, he may foretell before they come to passe, because he knowes them before hand by revelation and assignment from God.</u> Thus by the Witch of Endor, he foretold to Saul the time of his death and of his sonnes, and the ruine of his kingdome, saying, To morrow shalt thou and thy sonnes be with mee, and the Lord shall give the hosts of Israel into the hands of the Philistims; which particular event, and circumstance appertaining, he did truly define; not of himselfe, but because God had drawne away his good spirit from Saul, and had delivered him to be guided by the devil, whom he also appointed as a means, and used as an instrument to worke his overthrowe. The Scripture indeed maketh not particular mention of the time of Sauls death, it onely recordeth the manner thereof, and that which followed upon his death, the translating of the Kingdome to his neighbour David after him; <u>and yet because God used Satan as an instrument to bring this to passe, hereupon he was able to foretell the particular time when the will of God should be wrought upon him.</u> And these be the ordinary means and helps, whereby the devil may know and declare strange things, whether past, present, or to come. Neither may this seeme strange, that Sathan by such means should attaine unto\ such knowledge, for even men by their own observations may glue probable conjectures of the state and condition of sundry things to come. Thus we read, that some by observation have found out probably, and foretold the periods of families and kingdomes. For example, that the time and continuance of kingdoms is ordinarily determined at 500. yeares, or not much above: and the great similes have not gone beyond the six and seaventh generation. And as for special and private things, the world so runnes (as it were) in a circle, that if a man should but ordinarily observe the course of things, either in the weather, or in the bodies of men, or otherwise, he might easily foretell before hand what would come after. And by these and such like instances of experiences, men have guessed at the alterations and changes

43

[margin notes:] Does Satan still reside in God's court, then?

which would seem to indicate a certain cooperative relationship between God & Satan.

of estates, and things in particular. Now if men which be but of short continuance, and of a shallow reach in comparison, are able to doe such things, how much more easily may the Devil, having so great a measure of knowledge and experience, and being of so long continuance, having also marked the course of all estates, be able to foretell many things which are to come to passe? specially considering what the wise man hath set downe to this purpose, that that which hath been, shall be; and that which hath been done shall be done; and there is no new thing under the Sunne, Eccl.1.9. If it be here alleadged, that divination is a prerogative of God himselfe, and a part of his glory incómunicable to any creature, Isai. 41.23. I answer; Things to come must be considered two wayes; either in themselves, or in their causes and signes, which either goe with them, or before them. To foretell things to come, as they are in themselves, without respect unto their signes or causes, it is a property belonging to God onely; and the Devil doth it not by any direct and immediate knowledge of things simply considered in themselves, but onely as they are present in their signes or causes. Againe, God foretelleth things to come certainely, without the helpe of any creature, or other meanes out of himselfe; but the predictions of Satan are onely probable and conjectural; and when he foretelleth any thing certainely, it is by some revelation from God, as the death of Saul; or by the Scripture, as Alexanders victory; or by some speciall charge committed unto him, for the execution of gods will upon some particular places or persons, as before hath beene shewed. Thus much for the causes of Divination. Now follow the parts and branches thereof. Divination is of two sorts: either in and by meanes, or without meanes. Divination by meanes, is likewise of two sorts: either by such as are the true creatures of God; or those which are meerely counterfeit and forged. Sect. II. Divination by the true creatures of God, is distinguished according to the number of the creatures, into five distinct kinds, whereof four are mentioned in the Scriptures. § 1. The first, is by the flying and noise of birds.

Sorcerers among the heathen, used to observe foules in their flight; for example, whether they did slice on the right hand, or on the lest; above them, or below by them; whether crosse and overthwart, or directly against them. In like manner they observed the noise and sound of the sowle. And both these waies, sometimes by the noyse, and sometimes by the flight, they divined of things to come, both publike and private, of good and bad success in mans affairs; of the state of kingdóes, towns, families, and particular persons. Now this kind of divination is condemned by Moses, Deu. 18. 10. Let none be sound among you that is a--diviner of divination: that is, (as some interpret it) a marker of the flying of fowles: or a charmer, or a consulter with spirits, or soothsayer; that is, such a one as by observing the flying and noise of fowles, takes upon him to foretell good or bad succese. § 2. The second kind of creatures used for divination, are the intralls of beasts, of which mention is made, Ezech, 21. 21. where Nabuchadnezzar beeing to make warre both with the Jewes and the Ammonites, and doubting in the way which enterprise to undertake first, he offers a sacrifice to the Idol-gods; and opening the bellie of the sanctice, looks upon the liver, and by the signes therein found, hee judgeth what should be the issue of the warre. Which thing Nabuchadnezzar did according to the usuall practise of the Heathen, who when they were to make warre, or to attempt any busines of importance, were wont to offer sacrifice to their gods, and to prie into the intralls of the beast sacrificed: for example, the heart, stomak, splence, kidneys, but especially the liver, and by certain signes appearing in those parts, the devil was wont to reveale unto them, what should be the successe of their affaires they had in hand. It were easie to exemplifie both these sorts of Divination by sundry particulars out of Heathen writers; but seeing the Scripture hath manifested that there are such, and experience shews the same, I will forbear that labour, and proceede. But here it is demáded, why both these kinds of Divinatió should be condemned in Scripture, considering they had great applause

45

among the heathen? I answer, because the flying of birds, and the disposition of the inward parts of creaturs, as no true signs either of good or bad successe. For that which is a true signe of a future event, must have the Verte and power whereby it signifieth, from God himselfe, either by creation in the beginning, or by his speciall ordinance and appointment afterward. Now it cánot be shewed, that God in the creation infused any such vertue into the natures and motions of these creatures, whereby they might signifie such things; neither is there any apparant testimonie in the whole booke of the Scriptures, whereby it may be proofed, that since the creation, they were appointed by God, to serve such uses and cuds. And therefore howsoever they were esteemed of the Heathen, yet the word of God hath justly censured them, as no true and proper causes of Divination, sanctified by God, but meerely diabolicall. It is alleadged, that Joseph divided by his cuppe, as may appeare both by his stewards speech, as also by his owne, Gen. 44.5. and 15. and yet that cup received no power from God, either the one way or the other, to bee a cause or meane of divination. The answer anciently and commonly made is this; that Josephs steward spoke not as the thing was indeed, but as the common received opinion was among the Egyptians, who esteemed Joseph to be a man of great skill and wisedom, able by sundry means to divine and prophesie. To this I adde a second answer, that the steward spoke not as he thought, but his purpose was in those words, to conceal the knowledge of Joseph his master from his breathren, that thereby they might not discerne who hee was, but take him to be an Egyptian. Thirdly, the words may not unfitly admit this interpretation, as if the Steward had said, Know ye not that this cuppe which I find in the sacks mouth of your youngest brother, is that whereby my master will easily prove what manner of men you are? this answer is also ancient, and may well be received. It is further objected, that our Savior Christ by his speech unto the Pharises seemeth to approve of Divining by creatures, as by winds, and by clouds; When you see a cloud saith bee) rising out of the West, straight way you say, a shoure commeth, and so it is: and when you see the Southwind blow, ye say that it will be hoate, and it sommeth to passe, Luk. 12. 54. 55. Ans. There be some kinds of predictions that are and may be lawfully used, because they are naturall: of which sort are those that are made by Physitians, Mariners, and husbandmen, touching the particular alterations and dispositions of the weather; and these being agreable to that order which God hath set in nature from the beginning, by them a man may probably gather the state of the weather, whether it will be faire or foule; and of these naturall signes our Savior Christ speaketh, not of diabolicall, which have no warrant, either from the common course of nature created, or by any speciall appointment from God. So that what soever can be said in their defense, this yet remaineth certaine, that the flying and noise of birds, and the state of he intralls of beasts, are no true signes ordained by God, but invented by the devil and his instruments: and therefore all divination by them is justly condemned, as wicked and devilish. Whence it appeareth, what judgement may be given of those common signes of Divination, which are observed in the world, specially of the more ignorant fort. For example A man finds a peace of iron, he presently conceiveth a prediction of some good lucke unto himselfe that day. If he light on a peece of silver, then he stands contrarily affected, imagining some evil will befall him. Againe, when a man is taking of his journey, if a hare crosse him in the way, al is not well; his journey shall not be prosperous, it presageth some mischiefe towards him. Let his ears tingle or burne, hee is perswaded he hath enemies abroad and that some man either then doth, or presently will speake ill of him. If the salt fall towards a man at the table, it portendeth (in common conceit) some ill newes. When a raven stands upon some high place, looke what way he turnes himself and cries, thence, as some thinke, shall shortly come a dead corps; albeit this sometime may be true by reason of the sharpe sense of smelling in the raven. These and sundry other of the like fort, are meerely superstitious. For the truth is, they have no vertue in themselves to foreshewe any thing that is to come, either in nature, or by Gods ordinance. Therefore whatsoever divination is made by them, must needs be fetched from Satanical illusion. And though we cannot say they be soothsaying, or tearme the users and favourers of them Soothsayers, yet we may safely referre them to this kind of divining, being such as no Christian may warrantable use, though some of them be not so grosse and palpable, as those that are condemned in the Scriptures. § 3. The third kind of creatures used to divine by, are the starres. Divination by starres, is commonly called Indiciall Astrologie; of which we may reade, Deut. 18. 10. 11. where the holy Ghost doth of purpose reckon up all those kind of devilish arts, whereby men have dealings and society with Satan, either in divining or practising: among which this is the second. The word there used may carry a double sense. For it signifieth either him that observeth times, under which acception Astrologie is comprehended, or him that observeth the clouds. And howsoever the best learned Interpreters doe dissent about the notation of it, yet al agree in this, that this profession of Divining by the starres, is there condemned: and that it is to be numbred among the rest expressed in the prohibition, may further appeare by other places of Scripture, as in Isa. 47. 13. 14. where the Lord threatneth the same judgements against Diviners by the starres, that he doth against Soothsayers and Magicians. Againe, in Dan. 2.2. Inchanters, Astrologers, and Sorcerers are joyned together, as beeing all sent for about the same businesse, viz. to expound the Kings dreame. Now if the Lord himselfe have allotted the same punishment to the Astrologer, which he hath to the Soothsay and Magician, and account them all one; it is manifest, that Divining by the starres, ought to be held as a superslitious kind of Divination. Here, if it bee thought strange, that predictions by so excellent creatures as the stars be, should carrie both the name and nature of diabolicall practises, which can be done by none but such as are in league with Satan: I answer, The reasons hereof are these: First, it must be considered, that the drift and scope of this art, is to foretell the particular events of things contingent; as the alteration of the states of kingdomes, the deaths of Princes, good or badde successe of mens particular affaires, from the houre of their birth, to the day of their death. And from this all men may judge, what the are of it selfe is. For the foretelling of things so come, which in their owne nature are contingent, and in regard of us casuall (I say not in regard of God, to whome all things are certainely knowne) is a property peculiar to God alone, and not within the power of any creature, man, or Angell. A point that is plainely taught by the Prophet Isai, from the 4. chap. of his prophesie, to the 48. The scope whereof is to proove that it is a prerogative appropriated to the Deitie, and not communicable to the creature, to foreshew the event of things to come, which in our understanding and reach, may either be or not be; and which when they are, may be thus or otherwise. It remaines therefore, that Divinations of this kind, taking from God his right, and robbing him of his honour, are justly censured of impiety, and are in themselves wicked and abominable. It is alleadged, that stars in the heavens, are the causes of many things happening in the world, and therefore to practise by them in this manner, deserveth no such imputation. Ans. It cannot be denied that they are causes of some things: but I demand, what causes? not particular of particular events; but general and common, that worke alike upon all things: and no man can divine of a particular event, by a generall cause, unlesse he also know the particular causes subordinate to the general, and the particular dispositions and operations of them. For example, let twenty or thirty egges of sundry kinds of birds be taken and set under one and the same henne to be hatched; it is not possible for any man, onely upon the bare consideration of the heat of the hen, which is the generall cause of hatching the eggs, to set down certainely what kind of bird each egge will bring forth, unlesse he know what the egges were particularly. For a generall and common cause, doth not immediately produce a particular effect, but onely mooveth and helpeth the particular, immediate, and subordinate causes. Therefore the heat of the hen doth not make one egge to send forth a hen-chicken, another egge a ducke, a third a swanne, and c. but onely helpeth it forward by sitting and crouching upon them. In like manner the starres are generall causes of naturall things, as the heat of the hen is of the hatching of the egges, and by them no man can rightly define of particular events: and therefore Divination by the starres, whereby are foretold particular contingent events in kingdoms, similes, or particular persons, is but a forged skill, that hath no ground in nature fró the vertue of the starres, for any such purpose. A second reason may be this; All the rules and precepts of Astrologie, set down by the most learned among the Chaldeans Egyptians, and other Astrologers, are nothing else but meere dotages and fictions of the braine of man: for the rules and conclusions of all good and lawful arts, have their ground in experiece, and are framed by observation: wherupon they are called Axiomes, or positions of arte, so generally and undoubtedly true, that they cannot deceive. But these rules are of a contrary nature, having no foundation in experience at all: for if they had, this must needs follow, that the position of the heavens, and the course of all the starres, must needs continue one and the same; for the principles of art ought to be immutable: but neither the position of the heavens, nor the course of the starres, is alway one and the same. Againe, he that would make sound rules of art by observation, must know the particular estate of all things he observeth: But no man knoweth the particular estate of all the starres, and consequently none can gather sound rules of art by them. Thirdly, no man knoweth or seeth all the starres, and though they might be all discerned, yet the particular vertues of those which are seene, cannot be knowne, because their influences in the aire, and upon the earth are confused; and therefore by observation of them, no fules can be made, whereby to judge of particular events to come that be cótingent. But experience teacheth (may some say) that if a man addicted to this course shall practise the rules of Astrologie, it will fall out that the most things he for telleth shall be true, and come to passe accordingly: which beeing verified in experience, it should seeme, that these principles are not uncertain: for how is it possible that upon false grounds, should proceeds true predictions? To this objection, learned Divines have framed answer thus. That in this there is a secret Magicke at the least, if not an open league with Satan. For look what is wanting to the effect of the starres, the devil maketh supply of it by his owne knowledge, in things that are to come to passe. And this is the judgement of them that have knowne this art, which was also received for true in the daies of the Apostles. The third reason. The man that repaireth to the Astrologian upon the particular case for his helpe and counsell, must believe that he can and will doe for him; otherwise if he come doubting of his ability, or in way of tempting him, he cannot help him. Now in common understanding, if the diviner bring the thing to passe, here must needs be more then Art. For he that is a master of a lawfull art, can work by his rules, whether a man believe that he can er no; yea though all the men in the world should doubt, his rules would be effectuall. The art therefore it selfe is the old superstitious art of the Chaldeans, which they beeing Idolaters first fetched from the devil, and his Oracles: yea, the practise there of is nothing but superstitious sorcery, and the vndertakers no better then Sorcerers. If any man doubt hereof, their writings are sufficient testimony, and they théselves avouch it. For it is a rule and maxime among thé in all kind of Sorcerie, that the learner must come credulous, and not doubting, or to tempt; otherwise no answer can be given. But not withstanding all these reasons alleadged for the proofe of this point, sundry things are opposed to the contrary. For first, it is said that the Sunne, Moone, and starres were created for signes, Gen. 1. 14. and therefore that it is lawfull to divine by them, seeing that in so doing, we doe but use them to the end for which God made them. Ans. The reason is of no force. The starres indeed by this ordinance doe serve for signes, but of what? not of all things, but (as the text plainly sheweth) of daies, weekes, moneths, and yeares; yea, of the seasons of the yeare; as of Spring, Summer, Autumne, and Winter; yea further, of the alterations of the weather in generall: but all this maketh nothing to ratified Divination of particular events in things contingent, which are to fall out in the state of kingdomes, families, and persons: for they are not causes, but Signes, and that of some generall things onely, not of particular. Againe, it is said, that Moses and Daniel, two famous Prophets, are comméded for their skill in this art: for of Moses it is said, Act.7. 22. that he was learned in all the wisedome of the Egyptians: and Daniel in all the wisedome of the Chaldeans, Dan. 1. 17. 20. and we know that the Egyptians and Chaldeans were the masters of Divination, and eminent above all others in matters of Astrologie. Answ. It cannot be proofed out of those places, that Moses or Daniel were trained up in this art: and though it should be granted they were, yet it followes not, that they were practisers of it, at least continually. For albeit, being children and of tender years in the courts of Pharaoh and Nebuchadnezzar, they had bin trained up by their governours in this knowledge, it may not thence be concluded, that they finally submitted themselves to the practise thereof; considering that a man may learne that when he is young, which afterward upon better judgment and consideration, he may utterly disclaime. And so we are to thinke of them, that after God had called them, they did for ever lay aside all such wicked and devilish practises, forbidden by God, and yet in use among the Egyptians and Chaldeans. Thirdly, it is objected: the starres are admirable creatures of God, and the causes of many strange effects in the aire, in the waters, and upon the earth also, in the bodies of men and beasts: it may seeme therefore not unlawfull to divine by them. Ans. We graunt that the Starres, and especially the Sunne and Moone, have great vertue and force upon the creatures that are belowe; partly by their light, and partly by their heat; but hence it will not follow, that they are, or may be lawfully used for divination:

for whereas it hath been shewed, that the grounds of all good arts are gathered by observation and experience, it is not possible for any man, truely and certainly to observe all particular events brought forth by the starres, whereupon he might ground his rules. And for proofe hereof; Suppose there was a heap of all kinds of herbs growing upon the earth gathered together, which should be all strained into one vessel, and the liquor brought to the most skilfull Physitian that is, or ever was; can we think him able by tasting or smelling thereof, to distinguish the vertues of the hearbs, and to say which is which? To doe this when all are severed each from other, is a hard matter, yet possible, considering they have their severall natures and operations; but in this confused mixture to discerne the severalls is a thing passing the skill of man. The like may be said of the particular vertue of every starre; for they all have their operation in the bodies of men, and other creatures; but their vertues beeing all mixed together in the subject whereon they work, can no more be knowne distinctly, then the vertues of a masse of hearbs of infinite sorts beaten together. For this is an undoubted truth in nature: that the vertues of Celestial bodies, in their operations are mingled with the qualities of the elements in the inferiour bodies, and the vertues of them all doe so concurre, that neither the heate or light of the starres, nor the vertue of the elements, can be severed one from another. And therefore though there be notable vertue in the starres, yet in regard of the mixture thereof in their operation, no man is able to say by observation, that this is the vertue of this star, and this of that. The seaven planets beeing more notable, then the other lights of the heaven, specially the Sunne and Moone, have their operations and effects plainely and perfectly knowne; as for the other, there was never any man that could either feele their heate, or certainely determine of any thing by them. There beeing then some starres, whose vertues are unknowne, how can their operations and effects be discerned in particular? Therefore no rules can be made by observation of the vertues of the starres in their operations, wherupon we may foretell particular events of things contingent, either concerning mens persons, familíes, or kingdomes. A fourth reason, All starres have their work in the qualities of heate, light, cold, moisture, and dryness; as for the secret influences which men dreame of comming from them besides the said qualities, they are but forged fancies. The Scripture never mentioneth any such, neither can it be proofed that the Sunne hath any efficacie upon inferiour bodies, but by light and heate, which because they are mixt with other qualities, they afford no matter of prediction touching particular events. For what though the celestial bodies doe cause in the terrestriall, heate and cold, drought, and moisture? doth it therefore follow, that these effects doe declare before hand the constitution of mans bodie? the disposition of mens minds? the affections of mens hearts? or finally, what successe they shall have in their affaires, touching wealth, honor, and religion? Hence I conclude, that divining by them in this sort, is meere superstition, and a kind of Sorcery; for which cause in Scripture Astrologians are justly numbred among Sorcerers. Now that which hath been said touching this point, may serve for speciall use. And first, it gives a caveat to all Students, that they have care to spend their time and wits better, then in the study of Judiciall Astrologie; and rather imploy themselves in the searching out of such things, as may most serve for the glory of God, and the good of his Church. It is the subtilty of Sathan to drawe men into such meditations, and to make this study so pleasant, that it can hardly be left, when it is once begun: but let them take heed betime. For assuredly these vaine and superstitious practises, are not the builders and furtherers, but the hinderers and destroyers of religion, and the feare of God. Againe, this must admonish them which suffer any losses, not to seeke for helpe or remedy at the hands of Astrologers, commonly called Figure-casters: for their directions in the recovery of things lost or stollen, commeth not by the helpe of any lawfull art, but from the worke of the devil, revealing the same unto them. And better it were to loose a thing finally, and by faith to expect till God make supply another way, then in this manner to recover it againe: yea, the curse of God hangeth over the head of him, that to helpe himselfe useth diabolicall meanes. For put the case a thing lost of great value, be againe restored by the helpe of Satan; yet God in his justice, for the use of these unlawful means, may take from the Consulter twice as much; or at the least his grace, and so give him up to a reprobate sense, to believe the devil to his utter perdition. Thirdly, it serveth to admonish us of some other vanities that accompany Astrologie; especially of two. The first, is the observation of the signe in mans body; wherein not onely the ignorant sort, but men of knowledge doe farre overshoot themselves, superstitiously holding, that the signe is specially to be marked. An opinion in it selfe fantasticall and vaine, not grounded in nature, but borrowed from Astrologie. For the Astrologians for better expressing and establishing thereof, have devised new spheres in the heavens, more then indeede there be, to wit, the ninth and the tenth; and in the tenth commonly called the first mooneable, have placed an imaginary sphere, which they tearme the Zodiacke, and in the Zodiacke twelve signes, Aries, Taurus, Gemini, and the rest, which they imagine to have power over the twelve parts of mans body; as Aries, the head and face, Taur us necke and throat, and c. But these are onely twelue imaginary signes: for in the heavens there is no such matter as a ramme, a bull, and c. And how can it stand with reason, that in a firmament seigned by Pocts and Philosophers, a forged signe, which indeed is nothing, should have any power or operation in the bodies of men.

Againe, the very order of the government of these signes in mans body, is fond and without shew of reason. For according to this platforme, when the Moone commeth into the first signe, Aries, she ruleth in the head; and when she commeth into the second figne, Taurus, in the necke; and so descends down from part to part, in some part ruling two, in some three daies, and c. Where obserue, that the Moone is made then to rule in the cold and moist parts, when she is in hot and drie signes: when as in reason, a more consonant order were this; that when the Moone were in hot and dry signes, as Aries, Leo, and Sagittarius, she should rule in hot and drie parts of the body; and when she is in cold and moist signes, she should rule in the cold and moist parts of the body; and to still governe those parts, which in temperature come neerest to the nature of the signes wherin the Moone is. Besides this, some learned Physitians have upon experience confessed, that the observation of the signe, is nothing materiall, and that there is no danger in it, for gelding of cattell, or letting of blood. Indeed it prevailes oftentimes by an old conceit and strong imagination, on, of some unlettered persons, who thinke it to be of force and efficacie for restoring and curing; and yet the vanity of this conceit, appeares in the common practise of men, who commonly upon S. Stevens day use to let blood be the signe where it will; though it be in the place where the veine is opened. But the truth is, the signe in it owne nature, is neither way availeable, beeing but a fancie, grounded upon supposed premises, and therefore ought to be rejected, as a meere vanitie. The second thing belonging to Astrologie, which ought to be eschewed, is the choice and observation of dayes. Curious diviners doe set apart certaine dayes, whereof some are (as they say) lucky, some unlucky. And these they appoint to be observed for the beginning of ordinary works and businesses; as to take a journey, to beginne to lay a foundation of the building, to plant a garden, to weane a child, to put on new apparel, to flit into a new house, to trafficke into other countries, to goe about a suit to a Prince, or some great man, to hunt and use exercises, to pare the nailes, to cut the haire, in a word to attempt any thing in purpose or action, which is not done every day. The effect and force of these daies, is not grounded either in art or in nature, but onely in superstitious conceit and diabolical confidence, upon a wicked custome, borrowed from the practise of diviners: and the danger of such confident conceits is this; that the devil by them takes the vantage of fantastical persons, and brings them further into league and acquaintance with himselfe, unlesse they leave them. And all such persons as make difference of dayes for this or that purpose, are in expresse words plainly condemned, Deut. 18. 10. 11. 4. The fourth kind of Divination by true meanes, is the prediction of things to come by dreames. In the olde Testament we reade that Sorcerers and false Prophets used to foretell strange events, by revelations which they had in their dreames. Such diviners were among the Jewes; and for that cause the people of God were expressely forbidden to hearken unto Dreamers of Dreames, Deut. 13. 3. And the Lord himselfe by the Prophet Jeremie, taxeth the false Prophets, who broached false doctrine in his name by this devillish meanes, saying, I haus dreamed, I have dreamed, Jerem. 23. 25. Yet here it is to be remembred, that forctelling of future things by dreames, is not simply to be condemned, but onely in part. For of dreames there be three forts, Divne, Naturall, and Diabolicall. Divine, are those which come from God. Natural which proceed from a mans owne nature, and arise from the qualitie and constitution of the body. Diabolicall, which are caused by the suggestion of the devil. Touching Divine dreames; that there are, or at least have been such, it is evident. For these be the words of God, Num. 12. 6. If there be a Prophet of the Lord among you, I will bee knowne unto him by a vision, and will speake unto him by a dreame. And Job saith, that Ged speaketh in dreames and visions of the night when sleepe falleth upon men, and they sleepe upon their beds, Job. 33. 15. Now these divine dreames were caused in men, either immediately by God himselfe, as the former places shew; or by meanes of some good Angell. In this latter kind was Joseph often admonished in dreames what to doe, by the Ministery of an Angell; as Matth. 1. 20. and shap. 2. 13. 19. and divining by such dreams, is not condemned: for by them the most worthy Prophets of God have revealed Gods will in many things to his Church. Thus Joseph by dreame had notice given him of his owne advancement, Gen. 37. 7. 9. and by Pharaohs dreams which were sent from God, he also foretold the state of the kingdome of Egypt, touching provision for seaven yeares dearth, Gen. 41. 25. By the same meanes the Prophet Daniel prophesied of the flourishing and fading of the chiefe Monarchies of the world, from his time to the comming of Christ, Dan. 9. and c. These therefore beeing one of the extraordinary means, whereby God hath manifested his will unto man in times past, more or lesse; divination by them is not to be censured as unlawfull, but rather to be honoured and esteemed, as the ordinance of God. For the second fort which be Naturall, arirising either from the thoughts of the minde, or the affections of the heart, or the constitution of the bodie: as they are ordinary in all men, in some more, in some lesse; so they vary acording to the diversitie of mens thoughts, affections, and constitutions; and by them a man may probably conjecture of sundry things concerning the state and disposition, partly of his body, and partly of his mind. As first he may guesse in likelihood, what is his constitution, as the learned in all ages doe constantly avouch. For when his mind in dreaming runnes upon wars, and contentions, fire, and such like, it argueth his complexion is cholerike. When he dreams of waters and inundations, it betokeneth abundance of phlegme. When his fantasie conceiveth heavy and dolefull things, full of griese, feare, and horrot, it bewraieth a melancholike constitution. When his dreames be joyful and pleasant, as of mirth, pastimes, and delightfull newes; his complexion is judged to be sanguine. Againe, by naturall dreames a man may guesse at the corruption of his owne heart: and knowe to what sinnes he is most naturally inclined. For looke what men doe ordinarily in the day time conceive and imagine in their corrupt hearts, of the same, for the most part, they doe corruptly dreame in the night. And this is the rather to be observed, because though the wicked man shut his eyes, and stop his ears, and harden his heart, and will not take notice of his enormities by the light of the Law; yet even by his owne dreames in the night, his wickednesse shall be in part discovered, and his conscience there by convinced, and he himselfe left in the end inexcusable before God. Now albeit a man may probably conjecture of the premises by naturall dreames; yet no Divination of things to come, whether publicke or private, good or bad, can be made by them either concerning persons, families, or kingdomes. Therefore the common observations of dreams in the world, whereby men imagine things that are to come to passe, and accordingly foretell them by those meanes, are vaine and superstitious, and justly so condemned in the place before name, Deut. 13. Jer. 23. Concerning the third kinde of dreames, which are caused by the Devil. It hath beene granted in all ages for a truth, that Satan can frame dreames in the braine of a man, and by them reveal his divination. And it is plainely manifested by the continual observation of the Gentiles before the comming of Christ. For when Oracles, (that is, answers from the Devil,) were in force, men that used to consult with them, and desired to be resolved in matters of doubt, were to lay them downe and sleepe besides the altar of Apollo, where they had offered their gift; and sleeping they received in a dreame the answer for which they came; and this dreame was framed in the braine of him that slept, by the Devil, and in it the answer was deliver by him speaking at or in the Oracle. So likewise in the Primitive Church, since the comming of Christ, though Oracles then ceased, which were the greatest and strongest delusions that ever Sathan had; yet he hath by dreames and visions wrought in the heads of many men most strange and curious conceits for the raising up of heresies, to the great disturbance of the peace, of the Church. For we read in Ecclesiastical stories, that the Maniches had their damnable opiniñs first inspired into them, and then confirmed by dreames. And in this age the first authors of the sect of the Anabaptists, had their curious conceits of revelation, partly in dreams, partly in visions, Likewise the Family of love have their revelations in dreams. For he that desires to become one of that sect, must ascende thereunto by degrees, before he can come to perfection to be an elder illuminate, or a man deified; to which estate when he is once come, he hath for his conformation strong illusions, both waking and sleeping in visions and dreams. Histories of latter times, and wofull experience sheweth this to be true, the devil prevailing so strongly, that many have fallen away by this meanes, beeing corrupted by a doctrine merely carnall, howsoever maintained with great pretence of holines. Againe, as the good Angells may cause divine dreames from God, and therein reveale unto men his will and pleasure concerning things to come; so no doubt the evil spirits may cause in men diabolicall dreames, and therein reveale unto them many strange things; which they by means unknown to men, may foresee and know. By all which it is evident that there are and may be as well diabolicall dreames as divine dreames. The conclusion then is this: That as divided by the second sort is superstitious, having no ground from Gods word; so foretelling by this third fort is flat Witchcraft, directly condemned in the places forenamed, where men are forbidden to prophesie by them, or to regard them. Yet forasmuch as dreames be of sundry kinds, as hath been said, it shall not be amisse to set downe some notes of differences betweene them, whereby they may be known and distinguished each from other. Which point indeed bath long ago been handled in the Primitive Church, but hardly determined. For the learned of that age have avouched it a very hard matter, considering that the denill in these, as well as in other things, can transforme himself into an Angell of light. But howsoever the case be heard, and the devil politicke, yet by light of direction from the word of God, there may some true differences be set downe betweene them; as namely these. First of all; divine dreames have alwaies had their preeminence above others, that generally they have concerned the weightiest matters in the world; as the comming and exhibiting of the Messias; the changes and alterations of Kingdoms, the revealing of Antichrist, and the state of the Church of God. And this may plainly appeare by those which Joseph expounded unto Pharao, and Daniel unto the Kings of Babel and Persia. But in the other fort it is otherwise.

For if there be any thing represented more then ordinarie in those that be naturall, it proceedeth meerely from fancie and imagination. And as for diabolicall, they are not of so weighty matters, nor so hard to foretell. For though the Devil have great power and skill, yet it is above his reach to determine of such things as these are, or to foretell them without helpe from God. Secondly, divine dreames be alwaies either plaine and manifest, or if they be obscure yet they have a most evident interpretation annexed unto them. Of the plainer fort, were the dreames of Joseph the husband of Marie, Mar. 1. Of the other sort were Pharaohs very darke and hidden, but God raised up Joseph to give them an easie interpretation upon the instant. Gen. 41. Nebuchadnetsars dreames were full of obscurities, and many matters were contained in them, so as his spirit was troubled, and he forget them; but God stirred up Daniel and revealed to him the secret, so as he remembered it to the King, and declared the true meaning thereof, Dan. 2. 1. 28. 36. Lastly, Daniels dreames of the foure beasts, and c. were of like difficultie, but the Angel Gabriel was presently sent to make him to understand them, Dan. 8. 16. Now those that are caused by the Devil, as they be obscure and intricate, so the interpretation of them is ambiguous and uncertaine, because he himselfe cánot infallibly determine how things shall come to passe, and thereupon is constrained to give doubtfull answers by dreames. And such were not onely the ancient Oracles among the Heathen, where hee gave the resolution, but the modern Prophecies given by him to some of his instruments in the later time. Thirdly, the dreame that comes from God, is alwaies agreeable to his revealed will, and representeth nothing contrary to the same, in whole or in part: whereas those that proceed from nature, doe favour of nature, and be agreeable to mans corruption, which is repugnant unto Gods will. And those that are suggested by Satan, are of the same nature; the generall scope whereof is to crosse the will of God, and to withdrawe the heart from obedience thereunto. Fourthly, divine dreames ayme at this end, to further religion and piety, and to maintaine true doctrine: but the devil, an enemy to God, worketh in his dreames the subversion of true religion, and the worship of God, that in the roome thereof he may set up Idolatry and superstition. For so much we learne, Deut. 13. where the false Prophet brings his dreame, and utters it, yea and confitmeth it by a wonder; but marke his end: It was to drawe men to Apostacie; Let us (saith he) goe after other Gods, which thou hast not knowne, and let us serve them, vers. 2. Answerable to which, was the practise of the false prophets afterwards, who caused the people to erre by their lies and flatteries. Jer.23.32. To conclude this point, it must be here remembred, that howsoever there are and have been distinct sorts of dreames, yet those which are from God, were onely in ordinary use in the old Testament, and in the Church of the New are ceased, and take no place ordinarily. Whereas therefore men in their sleeps have dreames, they must take them commonly to be naturall, and withall know that they may be diabolicall, or mixt partly of the one kind, and partly of the other. And howsoever there may be some use of the naturall, as hath been said, yet commóly they are not to be regarded. And for the other which are from Sathan, or mixt, they are not to be received, believed, or made meanes wherby to foretell things to come; least by this use of them, we grow into familiarities with the devil, and before God be guilty of the sinne of Witchcraft. § 5. The fifth and last kind of Divination by true meanes, is by Lets; when men take upon the to search out fortune (as they use to speak) that is, good or bad successe in any business, by casting of Lots, whether it be by casting a die, or opening of a booke, or any such casuall meanes. I mention this the rather, because among the ignorant and superstitious sort, such practises are common and in great account: the Lot is an ordinance of

God, appointed for speciall end and purposes, but when it is that applied, it ceaseth to be lawfull, because it is abused to other ends then God by his word and ordinance hath allowed. That we may the better know the abuse of a Lot in this kind, we must remember there be three sorts of Lots; the Civil, the Sporting, and the Divining Lot. The civil use of Lots, is when they be used for the ending of controversies; the dividing of lands and heritages; the disposition of offices amongst many that are equally fit; the trying of the right in doubtfull things; or lastly, the discovery of a malefactor hid amógst many suspected. By this use of the Lot was Saul chosen to be King over Israel, 1. Sam. 10. 21. the skape-goate separated fró that which was to be sacrificed, Leuit. 16. 8. the land of Canaan divided among the children of Israel, Jos. 14. 2. and c. the trespasse of Achan found out, Josh. 7. 15. and Matthias chosen to be one of the twelve, Act. 1. 26. And of this Lot Salomon saith, Pro. 18. 18. The Lot causeth contentions to cease, and maketh partitions among the mightie. Hereupon the civil use of Lots hath his warrant in Gods word, so it be lawfully used in case of necessity, with invocation of the name of God, and with expectation of the event from God, by whose hand and immediate providence it is disposed. For the Lot (saith Salomon) is cast into the lappe, but the whole disposition thereof is from the Lord, Prov. 16. 33. The Sporting Lot is that which is commonly used for some vaine and unnecessary end; as to set up banck-rupts, or such like. This hath no warrant in the word of God whereupon men should use it, and therefore it is no better then an abuse of Gods ordinance, to speake no more of it. Now the divining Lot performed by the opening of a booke, or the casting of a die, or such like, thereby to declare good or bad successe, cannot be done without confederacie with Satan either explicite, or implicite. For the plain cast of a die, or the opening of a book without believing, can doe nothing for the discovering of future contingents. And what is there in the nature of these actions to produce such effects? or where, or when did God give this vertue to them certainly to determine of things hidden from man, and known onely to himselfe? Divination therefore by them is to be holden as a practise, not onely favouring of superstition, but proceeding from the arte of Witchcraft and Sorcerie. And thus much of Divination, by means of the creatures; and the several kinds thereof. Sect. III. The second kind of Divination, is by counterfeit and forged meanes, which are none of the creatures of God: where of one kinde onely is mentioned in Scripture, viz, when Satan is cósulted with in the shape of a dead man. This is commonly called Necromancie, or the blacke art, because the devil being sought unto by Witches, appeares unto them in the likenesses of a dead bodie. And it is expressely forbidden Deut. 18. 11. yea condemned by the Prophet Esay, 8. 19. 20. who saith in plaine tearmes, that Gods people ought not to goe from the lisling to the dead, but to the Lawe and to the testimonie. A memorable example hereof is recorded in 1. Sam. 28. the observation whereof will discover unto us the chiefe points of Necromancie. There Saul about to encounter the Philistims, beeing forsaken of God, who refused to answer him, either by dreames, or by Urim, or by the Prophets, inquired for one that had a familiar spirit: and hearing of the Pythonesse at Endor, went unto her by night, and caused her to raise up Samuel, to tell him the issue of the warre. Now the Witch at his request raised up the Devil, with whom she was confederate, in Samuels likenesse; who gave him answer, concerning his owne overthrow, and the death of his sonnes. Which example declareth plainely that there is a kind of divination, whereby witches and sorcerers reveal strange things, by meanes of the devil appearing unto them in the shapes or shadowes of the dead. Touching the truth of this example, two Questions may be mooved. The first is, Whether that which appeared was true Samuel or not? Some say it was Samuel indeed: others (who hold that there are no Witches) denie that it was either Samuel, or the devil; and affirme it to be some other counterfeit comming in Samuels attire to deceive Saul: both which opinions are false, and here to be confuted. And first, that their opinion which say that true Samuel appeared vnto Saul, is a flat untruth, I proove by these reasons. I. Before this time, God had withdrawne his spirit from Saul, as himselfe confesseth, and denied to answer him any more by ordinarie meanes, in such sort as before hee had done. Hereupon I gather, that it was not probable, that God would now vouchsafe him the favour to suffer Samuel to come unto him extraordinarily, and tell him what should be the end of his warre with the Philistims: and to this purpose it is affirmed twice in that Chapter, that God had taken his good spirit from Saul. II. The foules of the faithfull departed, are in the hand of God, and doe rest in glory with himselfe, and their bodies are in the earth, and there rest in peace. So saith the voice from heaven, Revel. 14. 13. Blessed are the dead that die in the Lord: for they rest from their labours, and their workes, that is, the reward of their works, follow them immediately, or at the heeles, as the word signifieth. Now suppose the devil had power over Samuels bodie, yet to make true Samuel, he must have his soule also. But it is not in the power of the Devil, to bring againe the soules that are in heaven unto their bodies, and so to cause them to appeare unto men upon earth, and to speake unto them. The Devils kingdome is in hell, and in the hearts of wicked men on earth; yea whiles the children of God are in this world, he usurpeth some authority over them, by meanes of their owne corruption: But heaven is the kingdome of God and his Saints, where Satan hath nothing to doe, considering that there is no flesh or corruption, to make him entrance or yield him entertainment. Neither can it be proofed by Scripture, that the Devil can disturbe either the bodies or soules of them that die in the Lord: and therefore the Witch with all her power and skill, could not bring Samuels rotten body (for so no doubt it was now) and soule together. III. This shape which appeared, suffered Saul to adore and worship it, whereas the true Samuel would never have received adoration from Saul the King, though it had beene in civil manner onely. Whom then did Saul adore? Ans. The Devil himselfe, who beeing an enemie to the glorie of God, was content to take to himselfe that honour, which a King in dutie is to performe to God himselfe. IV. If it had beene true Samuel, he would certainly have reprooved Saul for seeking help at witches, contrary to Gods commandement, and that doctrine which hee had taught him from God in his life time. But this counterfeit reprooved him not, and therefore it is not like to be the true Prophet of God, but Satan himselfe, framing by his art and skill the person and shape of Samuel. But it is alledged to the contrary, that Samuel after his sleep, prophecies of the death of Saul, Ecclesiastic. 46.iv.20. After his sleepe also be told of the Kings death, and c. Answ. That booke penned by Jesus the sonne of Sirach is a very worthy description of Christian Ethicks, conteining more excellent precepts for manners, then all the writings of heathen Philosophers or other men. But yet it is not Scripture, neither did the Church ever hold and receive it as Canonicall; yea, the author himselfe insinuateth so much in the beginning thereof, for in the preface he disableth himselfe to interpret hard things, and after a sort craves pardon for his weaknes, which is not the manner of the men of God, that were penmen of Scripture. For they were so guided by Gods spirit in their proceedings, that nothing could be hard unto them. This priviledge no ordinary man hath assurance of: and therefore this author writing upon his owne private motion, was subject to error, and no doubt the speech of his, beeing contrary to that which is-recorded in the Canonicall Scriptures, is a flat untruth. Secondly, it is objected, that the Scripture calleth him Samuel, that appeared unto Saul. Ans. The Scripture doth often speak of things, not as they are in themselves, but as they seeme to us. So it is affirmed, Gen. 1.16. that God made two great lights, the Sunne and the Moone; whereas the moone is lesser then many starres, yet because in regard of her nearnesse to the earth, shee seemeth unto us greater then the rest, therefore shee is called a great light. In like manner Idols in the Scripture are called Gods, not that they are so indeed, (for an Idoll is nothing, 1. Cor. 8.4.) but because some men doe so conceive of them in their mindes. In a word; the Scripture oftentimes doth abase it selfe to our conceit, speaking of things not according as they are, but after the manner of men; and so in this place calleth counterfeit Samuel, by the nature of the true Samuel, because it seemed so unto Saul. The third objection; That body which appeared, prophecies of things that came to passe the day after, as the death of Saul, and of his sonnes; which indeed so fell out, and at the same time, therefore was like to be Samuel. Answ. There is nothing there said or done, which the devil might not doe. For when the Lord useth the devil as his instrument to bring some things to passe, he doth before hand reveile the same unto him; and looke what particulars the devil learneth from God, those he can foretell. Now the truth is, Satan was appointed by God to worke Sauls overthrow, and it was made knowne unto him when the thing should be done; by which meanes, and by none other, the devil was enabled to foretell the death of Saul. Where (by the way) observe, that in this case the devil can reveale things to come certenly, to wit, if hee be appointed Gods immediate instrument for the execution of them, or knows them by light of former prophecies in Scripture. Fourthly, dead men doe often appeare and walke after they are buried. Ans. It is indeed the opinion of the Church of Rome, and of many ignorant persons among us: but the truth is otherwise. Dead men doe neither walke nor appeare in body or soule after death: for all that die, are either Righteous or wicked: The soules of the righteous goe straight to heaven, and the soules of the wicked to hell, and there remaine till the last judgment: and therefore of the just it is said, that they are blessed when they die, because they rest from their labours; Apoc.14.13. But how doe they rest, if after they be dead they wander up and dowse in the earth? If it be said, that Moses and Elias appeared when Christ, was transfigured in the Mount; and that Lazarus rose againe, and at Christs resurrection many dead bodies rose againe and appeared. I answer; there were two times when God suffered the dead to be raised up againe; either at the planting of his Church, or at the restoring and establishing of it, when it was rased to the foundation. Thus at the restoring of religion in Elias and Elishas times, the sonne of the Shunamitish woman, 2. King.4.34. and the widowes sonne at Sarephta, 1. King.17.21. were raised. Againe, when God would restore his Church which was fallen to Idolatry about the death of Elisha, he caused the like miracle to be wrought in the reviving of a dead man by the touching of Elishas dead carkeise in the grave, thereby to assure the people of their deliverance, and to cause them to embrace the doctrine of the Prophet after his death, which in his life they had contemned. In like manner at the establishing of the Gospel in the new Testament, it pleased Christ to raise up Moses and Elias, and to make them knowne to his Disciples by extraordinary revelation, that they might believe that the doctrine which he preached was not new, but the same in substance with that which was recorded in the Law and the Prophets, both which were represented by Moses and Elias. So also he wrought the miracle upon Lazarus, the widowes sonne, and Jairus daughter, thereby to shew the power of his Godhead, the truth of his calling, the testimony of his doctrine: lastly, to make knowne the power of his resurrection, he caused some to rise and appeare to others, when he himselfe rose againe. But out of these two times we have neither warrant nor example, that God suffered the dead to be raised up. Wherefore those instances will not any way confirme Samuels appearing, which indeede was not true, but counterfeit and forged by the Devil himselfe. Now for the Second Opinion, of those which denie that there be any Witches, and there up on hold that this was a meere cozenage of the Witch, suborning some man or woman to counterfeit the forme, attire, and voyce of Samuel, thereby to delude Saul; that also is untrue. For he that spake foretold the ruine of Saul, of his sonnes, and of his army, yea the time also wherein this was to come to passe: whereas in likelihood no man or woman in al Israel, could have foretold such things before hand of themselves. It was not then any cozenage, as is affirmed, but a thing effected by the devil, framing to himselfe a body in the likenesse of Samuel, wherein hee spake. If therefore it be manifest, that by counterfeit apparitions of the dead, Witches and Sorcerers can foretell things to come: hence sundry points of Witchcraft may be observed. First, that there is a league betweene the Witch and the devil. For this was the cause which mooved Saul to seeke to Witches, because neither he himselfe, nor any of his servants could raise up Satan in Samuels likenes, as the Witch of Endor did. But Saul beeing a King, might have commanded helpe from all the wise and learned men in Israel, for the effecting of such a matter: why then would he rather seeke to a silly woman, then to them? The reason was, because she had made a compact with the devil, for the using of his helpe at her demand, by vertue whereof he was as ready to answer, as she to call him; whereas Saul and the learned Jews, having made no such league, neither he by his power, nor they by their skill, could have performed such a worke. Secondly, the devil will be ready at the call and command of Witches and Sorcerers, when they are intending any mischiefe. For here the Witch of Endor no sooner spake, but he appeared: and therefore the text gives her a name that signifieth, one having rule and command over Pytho, that is, the familiar spirit: yet when he is cómanded, he yields not upon constraint but volútarily, because he builds upon his own greater advantage, the gaining of the soule of the Witch. Where by the way, let it be observed, what a previous thing the soule of man is; the purchasing whereof, can make the proud spirit of Satan so farre to abase it selfe, as to be at the command of a silly woman. Againe, what an inveterate malice Satan beareth to man, which for the gaining of a soule, will doe that which is so contrary to his nature. It may teach man what to esteeme of his soule, and not to sell it for so base a price. Thirdly, by this, the great power of the devil in the behalfe of the Sorcerer, is made manifest. For he was presently at hand to counterfeit Samuel, and did it so lively and cunningly, as well in forme of body, as in attire and voice, that Saul thought verily it was the Prophet: which may be a caveat unto us, not easily to give credit to any such apparitions. For though they seeme never so true and evident, yet such is the power and skill of the devil, that he can quite deceive us, as he did Saul in this place. Sect. IV. Hitherco I have shewed the first kinde of Divination by means, both true and forged. Now followeth the secód; practised without means. Divination without meanes, is the foretelling and revealing of things to come, by the alone and immediate assistance of a familiar spirit. This kind is mentioned, and expressely forbidden, Leuit. 19.31. Ye shall not regard them that worke with spirits. Againe, Leuit.20.6. If any turne after such as worke with spirits, to goe a whoring after them, I will set my face against that person, and will cut him off from among his people. So Deut.18.11. Let none be sound among you, that consulteth with spirits. In which places the holy Ghost useth the word Ob, which more properly signifieth a spirit, or devil: in which sense it is taken in Leuit. 20.27. and in 1.Sam.28.8. And by reason of the league which is between the Witch and the devil, the same is also given to the Witch, that worketh by the devil: and therefore the Pythonesse at Endor, is both called Ob, 1.Sam.28.9. and she that ruleth Ob.v.7.8. Now this kinde of Divination is practised two wayes: either inwardly, when the spirit is within the Witch: or out wardly, when beeing forth of the Witch, he doth onely inspire him or her. An example of the former way, the Scripture affoardeth, Act. 16. 16. of a woman at Philippi, that had a spirit of Pytho; which gat her master much vantage with divining. And this spirit whereby she divined was within her. For Paul beeing molested, said to the spirit, I command thee in the name of Jesus Christ, that thou come out of her; and he came out of her the same houre, v. 18. And because the devil is not wót in this kind to speak out of the throat and brest, or belly of the Witch possessed, hereupon learned men have thought that this name (Ob) is given to the devil, because he speaketh out of the Witch as out of a bottle or hollow vessell; for so the word Ob, properly signifieth.

Secondly, this may be practised when the devil is forth of the Witch; and then he either inspireth her, or else casteth her into a trance, and therein revealeth unto her such things as she would know. Of this kind, though we have no example in Scripture, yet the histories of the Heathen doe afford unto us many instances of experiece therein. One of the principall is the history of the tenne Sibylles of Greece, who were most famous Witches, and did prophecie of many things to come, where of some were true concerning Christ and his king dome, which the devil stole out of the Bible, and some other were false: and all of them they received by revelation from the devil in trances.

But it will be said, if the devil reveileth unto his instruments strange things in trances, then how shall a man discerne between diabolicall revelations, and the true gift of Prophecie; which God in trances reveileth unto his Prophets. Ans. In this point Satan is (as it were) Gods ape: For as he in olde time raised up holy Prophets to speake unto the fathers, for the building up of his Church: so hath Satan inspired his ministers, and furnished his instruments with propheticall inspirations from time to time, for the building up of his own kingdom: and hereupon he hath notably counterfeited the true gift of prophecie received first from God himselfe. And yet, though in many things they be like, there is great difference between them. First, divine trances may come upon Gods children, either when the soule remaineth united with the body, or else when it is severed for a time. So much Paul insinuateth, when he faith of himselfe, 2. Cor. 12.2. that he was rapt up (as it were in a heavély trance) into the third heaven, but whether in the body, or out of the body, he knew not. But in all diabolicall ecstasies, though the body and senses of the Witch be (as it were) bound or benummed for the time; yet their soules still remaine united to their bodies, and not severed from them. For though the devil by Gods permission may kill the body, and so take the soule out of it for ever; yet to take it from the body for a time, and to reunite them againe, is miraculous, and therefore beyond the compasse of his power. Secondly, in divine trances the servants of God have all their senses, yea and all the powers of soule and body remaining sound and perfect, only for a time the actions and operations are suspended and cease to doe their duty: but in ecstasies that be from Satan, his instruments are cast into frenzies and madnesse:so as reason in them is darkened, understanding obscured, memorie weakened, the braine distempered; yea all the faculties are so blemished, that many of them never recover their former estate againe, and they that scape best, doe carrie their blemishes, as the devils scars, even to their grave. So kind is Satan to his friends, that he will leave his tokens behind him where ever he comes in this sort. The servants of God receive no such blemish, but rather a further good, and a greater measure of illumination of all the powers of the soule. Thirdly, divine ecstasies tend always to the confirming of the truth of the Gospell, and the furtherance of true religion and piety. Such was Peters, Act. 10. 11. which served to assure him of his calling to preach the Gospell to the Gentiles, and to informe his judgment in this truth, that there was no acception of persons with God, and that to them of the new Testament, all things cleane, and nothing polluted. But the scope of them that are from Satan, is principally the suppressing and hindrance of religion, the drawing of the weake into errours, the ratifying and confirming of them that are fallen there into, and the generall upholding of the practices of ungodlines. And by these and such like particular differences, hath God pulled off the Devils vicar, and made him better known and discerned of true Christians. And thus much concerning Divination, the first part of Witch-craft.

CHAP. IV.

Of operatiue or working Witch-craft.

THe second part is that which consisteth in Operation, and is therefore called Operative or working Witchcraft. Witch-craft in Operation, is that which is employed in the practise and reall working of strange things or wonders, and it hath two parts, Inchantment, and Jugling. Sect. I. Inchantment is the working of wonders by a charme. This the Lord expressely forbiddeth, Deut, 18. 11. Let none bee found among you, that is a Charmer. In this description, two points are to be considered:1. what things may be done by inchantment, namely wonders, for I say it is the practise of wonders: 2. by what meanes these wonders are wrought, that is, by a Charme. For the first: The wonders done by Inchanters are, 1. The raising of stormes and tempests; windes and weather, by sea and by land: 2. The poysoning of the ayre: 3. Blasting of corne: 4. Killing of cattle, and annoying of men, women, and children: 5. The procuring of strange passions and torments in mens bodies, and other creatures, with the curing of the same:6. Casting out of Devils. These and such like things Inchanters can doe by their charmes. And for proofe hereof, we have the uniforme consent of all ages, with the records of Witches confessions to manifest the same; besides the testimony of experience in this age: so as the man that calls it into question, may as well doubt of the Sunne shining at noone day. Yet for the further declaration thereof, we will alleadge what the Scripture saith in this point. Salomon saith, If the Serpent bite when he is not charmed, no better is a babler, Eccles.10.11.thus the words are in our English translation: but they may be better thus read according to the originall: If the serpent bite before he be charmed, what profit hath the master of the tongue thereby, that is, the Charmer. And so they beare this sense. If the Inchanter be bitten, before the serpent be charmed, then he hath no benefit by his charme. For Salomon in that place giveth us to understand, what power Inchanters have, and what they may doe by their charmes, if they come in time, namely, stay the poison of the serpent, so as he cannot hurt, either by biting or stinging. When Balac intended evil against Israel, he hired Balaam to curse thé Num. 22.6. Now this Balaam was an inchanting Witch; for though he be called a Prophet, yet this was onely in the reputation of the world; for his practise was to inchát by charms of words; and to that purpose he was hired to curse Gods people, that is, to bring mischeife upon them by charming; which thing when he had often and many waies affaied to doe, and could no way prevaile, but that it pleased God contrary to his endeavours, to blesse Israel, the he breakes out into these words, There is no sorcerie against Jacob, nor soothsaying against Israel, Num. 23. 23. As if the should have said, I know well that sorcerie is powerfull in many things, and of force to bring much mischiefe upon men, yet it can take no place against the people of God, because he hath blessed them; and whole he blesseth, them no man can hurt by cursing. Inchanters therefore, may upon Gods permission works strange things, as appeares by these places, to name no more. The second point to be observed, is the meanes whereby these wonders are practised; these are counterfeit and supposed meanes, not ordeyned and sanctified by God, which are commonly called Charmes. A Charme is a Spell or verse, consisting of strange words, used as a signe or watchword to the devil, to cause him to worke wonders. First, I say it is a Spell consisting of strange words, because in these inchantments, certaine words or verses are secretly uttered, which in regard of the common formes of words are strange, and wherein there is thought to be a miraculous efficacie to bring some extraordinary and unexpected thing to passe. A point of it selfe evident and needing no further proofe, considering it is not unknowne to the more ignorant sort, who are better acquainted with these, then with the word of God. And these words are not all of one and the same kind; but some are rude and barbarous, neither knowne nor conceived or understood; of which the aneienter fort of Charmes were wont to be made especially, and some later. Some againe are plaine and knowne tearmes, which may be understood; as the names of the Trinitie, some words and sentences of Scripture, as In princicipio arat verbum, and c. Again, charmes that cousilt of words, are not all of one sort, but some be imprecations, wishing some evil: others in shew have the forme of praises and blessings, whereby the Witch either flatteringly commendeth, or favourably wisheth some good: others againe are made in forme of prayer and petition: and they all are sometimes plainely conceived, sometimes in ruder and more unknown words, as those wel know, who have heard them, or read them where they are to be found. Secondly, I adde, that the charme is used for a signe and watchword to the devil, to cause him to worke wonders, wherein standeth the nature and proper end of a Charme. The nature, in that it is a diabolicall signe; the end, to cause the devil to worke a wonder: whereby it is distin-guished from all other speaches of men. For all they commonly carry the nature of the thing, whereof and whereabout they be made, but the Charme doth not alwaies follow the nature of the words, but hath another nature in regard of the immediate revelation it hath to the devil, to whom it is a signe. Againe, the charme pronounced doth not the wonder, but the devil admonished by it as by the watch-word to doe the feate. Now because some are of opinion, in regard of the ordinary production of strange effects by these meanes, that the Spell hath in it selfe some vertue and power to such and such purposes whereunto it is used; I will stand a little in the proofe of the contrarie. That a Charme is onely a diabolicall watchword, and hath in it selfe no such effectuall power or possibilitie to worke a wonder. My reasons are these. First, this must be taken for a maine ground; That as there is nothing in the world, that hath being but from God, so nothing hath in it any efficacie, but by his ordinance. Now what soever efficacie, is in any creature from God, it received the same into it selfe, either by creation, or since the creation by some new and speciall institution, appointment, and gist of God. For example. The bread in the Sacrament, by a naturall power given unto it in the creation, serveth to nourish the bodie; and the same bread, by Gods speciall appointment in his word, feedes the soule, in that by his ordinance it is made to us a signe and seale of the body of Christ broken for us: And so it is in every creature; if the effect be ordinary and naturall, it hath it by creation; if extraordinarie and supernatural, it hath that by divine ordinatió: So that whatsoever comes to passe by any other meanes, is by Satanicall operation. Now Charmes and Spells, standing of set words and sillables, have no power in them to worke wonders, either by the gift of nature in the creatió, or by Gods appointment since the creation: and therefore they have in them no power at all for any such purpose. This latter part of the reason, beeing the assumption or application of the ground to the present instance, consisteth of two parts, which I will proove in order. First then I affirme, that by the gift of nature, no words of Charmes have power in them to worke wonders; and I proove it in this manner. I. All words made and uttered by men, are in their owne nature but sounds framed by the tongue, of the breath that commeth from the lungs. And that which is onely a bare sound, in all reason can have no vertue in it to cause a reall worke, much lesse to produce a wonder. The sounds of bells and of many musicall instruments, and the voices of many bruit creatures, are farre more strong and powerfull then the voice of a man: yet who knoweth not, that none of all these is availeable to such purposes. Indeed they have power to affect the minde, by their sweetnesse or otherwise, but they are not able to bring to passe a reall worke, either by the inflicting of hurts and harmes, or by the procuring of good. I conclude therefore, that the voice of man by nature, hath no power to worke any wonders. II. Againe, every thing which hurteth or affecteth another, must necessarily touch the thing which it hurteth or affecteth. For it is a granted rule in nature, that every agent worketh upon the patient by touching: But words uttered in Charmes are commonly made of things absent, and therefore though it should be granted, that they had the power of touching a substance (which they cannot have) yet of themselves they are not available to bring upon things absent good or bad. III. Moreover, if wordes conceived in charmes and spells have any such power as is pretéded, why should not every word that any man speaketh have the same power, inasmuch as all words are of the same nature, beeing only sounds framed in the breast, and uttered of the tongue in letters and syllables? But experience teacheth, that the same word spoken by another, hath not the same vertue? For the charme uttered by the Charmer himselfe, will take effect, but being spoken in the same manner by another man, that is no Inchanter, maketh to no purpose, for nothing is effected by it. IV. That which is in nature nothing but a bare signification, cannot serve to worke a wonder, and this is the nature of all words; for as they be framed of mans breath, they are natural, but yet in regard of forme and articulation they are artificiall and significant, and the use of them in every language is, to signifie that which the author thereof intended: for the first significations of words, depended upon the will and pleasure of man that framed and invented them. Beeing therefore invented onely to shew or signifie some thing, it remaines that neither in nature nor proper use, they can be applyed to the producing of wonderfull and strange effects. Thus the former part of the assumption is cleared. In the second place I affirme, that the words of charmers have not this power in them, by any speciall gift, blessing, or appointment of God, since the creation, which is the other part of the assumption. And I shew it thus: whatsoever is powerfull and effectuall to any ende or purpose, by Gods gift, blessing, or appointment, the same is commanded in his word to be used, and hath also a promise of blessing annexed to the right use thereof. To use the instance before made for explanation sake. The bread in the Lords supper, hath this power and property given it by Christ: to seale and signifie unto every believing receiver the Body of Christ; and by this property given it, it is available to this purpose; though it be a thing above the common and naturall use of bread; and thereupon we have warrant from Christs own commandment, ordinance, and example so to use it. But in the whole body of the Scripture, there is not the like commandment to use the words of Charmes for the effecting of wonders, much lesse the like promise of blessing upon the same so used: therefore the conclusion is, that God hath given no such power unto them in speciall. If it be asked then, what they are, and whereto they serve? I answer, they are no better then the devils sacraméts and watchwords, to cause him to do some strange worke. For the Inchanter hath relation in his minde to the devil, whose helpe he hath at hand by covenant either open or secret; or at least some superstitious opinion of the force of the words, which is a preparation to a covenant. The truth of this doctrine, howsoever it be thus made manifest, yet it findes not generall intertainment at all mens hands. For there are and have been some learned men, in all ages, who maintained the contrary, both by word and writing; and namely that there is great vertue and power in words pronounced in time and place, to effect strange things. For proofe whereof they alleadge these reasons. First, that the bare conceit and imagination of man, is of great force to doe strange things; and therefore words expressed much more. Ans. The ground of the reason is naught. Imagination is nothing else but a strong conceit of the minde touching any thing, whatsoever it be, and by reason of the communion that is between the body and soule being together, it is of great force to worke within the man that imagineth diversely, and to cause alteration in himselfe, which may tend either to the hurt or to the good of his own body: but yet imagination hath no force out of a man to affect or hurt an other. A man (conceiving desperately of his own estate) by the strength of imagination may kill himselfe; but the same conceit, be it never so strong, can not hurt his neighbour. For it is no more then Cæsars image upon his coyne, which serveth only to represent Cæsar: so imaginatió is nothing but the represétation of some thing in the mind by conceit; and therefore as the person of Cefar is nothing hurt, though his image be defaced; so when we conceive of men in our minds, though never so badly and malitionsly, yet al is of no force to hurt or annoy them, either in person or state. Secondly, they alleadge that Witches by malitious and wrie lookes, in anger and displeasure, may and doe hurt those upon whom they looke, whether they be men or other creatures. And it is an old received opinion, that in malitious and ill disposed persons, there proceed out of the eye with the beames, noysome and malignant spirits, which infect the ayre, and doe poison or kill, not onely them with whom they are daily conversat, but others also whose company they frequent, of what age, strength, and complexion soever they be. Ans. But the opinion is as fond, as it is old: for it is as much against nature that such vertue should proceed out of the eye, or such spirits breake out of the nerves to the party hated, as it is for the blood of the body, of it selfe, to gush out of the veines. Yet for the ratifying of this opinion, they alledge that which is writté in Gen. 30. 37. where Jacob had speckled roddes before the sheepe in their watery troughes, and that by Gods appointment, for this end, that they might bring forth party-coloured lambs. I answer, that was not a work of sight, but a speciall and extraordinary worke of Gods providence upon Jacob in his necessitie, as we may plainely see in the chapter next following, v. 9. and 11. yea it was taught Jacob by God himselfe; and if it had been an ordinarie worke, doubtlesse the gaines thereof beeing so good, Jacob would have done it againe afterward; but we never reade that he did it againe. And be it granted it were a naturall worke, yet it cannot proove witching by sight, because the sheepe received into their eyes the species and resemblance of therods, which is according to nature; whereas in fascination or bewitching by sight, malignant spirits should not be received in, but sent forth of the eye, which is against nature. Yea, but the Basiliske or, Cockatrice doth kill man and beast with his breath and sight, yea the wolfe takes away the voyce of such as he suddenly meetes withall and beholds, and why may not wicked men or women doe the like? Ans. Indeed it is a thing received by common errour, and held of some for a truth; but no experience of any man hath yet been brought for the proofe thereof, and therefore it is to be reputed as fabulous. Thus much in probability may be thought (if the allegatió should be true) that the Basiliske being possessed of a thicke poyson, may by his breath send forth some grosse venomous vapours, and thereby infect the ayre, and poison the thing that is neere unto him. Againe, that the suddoine and unexpected beholding of the venemous Cockatrice, or the ravenous wolfe, (being creatures in their kind fearefull, especially to these that are not acquainted with thé) may cause present astonishmét, and consequently perill of death. But that this should be done by the eyes of these creaturs only, in manner aforesaid, it is not credible; and therfore Authors have upon good ground denied it, as beeing confirmed neither by reason, nor experience. Thirdly, they reason thus; Inchanters by whispering of words in charmes can stay the stinging and poisoning of serpents; for so David in effect speaketh, that the voice of the Charmer charmeth the serpent, Psal. 58. 5. It may seeme therefore that there is no small force in words for the effecting of strange workes. Ans. It must be granted that the Charmer may inchant the serpent: but how? not by vertue of the words in the Charme, but by power of the devil, who then is stirred up, when the charme is repeated, to doe the thing intended. The truth of this answer appears by the words of the text, as they are reade in the originall, that the Inchanter joyneth societies very cunningly, namely, with the Devil. Now these societies betweene Satan and the Charmer, are the very ground of the work upon the serpent: which worke upon confederacies formerly made, is done by the devil, and the words of the Charme are no more but the Inchanters Item or watchword, to occasion him thereunto. And let any other man repeate the same words a thousand times, that either is not thus confederate with Satan, or hath not a superstitious opinion of Charmes, and all his labour will be in vaine. Fourthly, the word of God is of great force in the hearts of men to convert and change them, as it is uttered by the mouth of mortall man: and this force is not in the man by whom it is spoken; where then should it be, but in the words? and then if in the words, why may not other words be of like efficacie, beeing uttered by man? Ans. 1. The power of Gods word commeth not from this, that it is a word, and barely uttered out of the mouth of a man; for so it is a dead letter: but it proceedeth from the powerfull operation of the spirit, annexed by Gods promise thereunto, when it is uttered, read, and conceived; which operation if it were taken away, the word might be preached a thousand years together, without any fruit or effect, either to salvation or condemnation. 2. The word of God is powerful by the concurrence of the worke of the spirit, not in all things; as for example, in raising winds and tempests, in infecting the ayre, in killing and annoying men or other creatures; but in the conversion of sinners, in gathering the elect, and in confirming those that be called: and this power it hath also by his speciall blessing and appointment. 3. Furthermore, the same word is not of power, when it is barely read, heard, or spoken, unless it be also conceived in the understáding, received with reverence, treasured up in the memory, and mingled with faith in the heart: whereas the bare reading and muttering over the words of a Charme by an Incháter, though in an unknowne tongue, in rude and barbarous words, is sufficient to procure the working of wonders. Now though the word of God be in it selfe pure, and serve to excellent purpose, as hath been said, yet by the way we may remember; That as it is with all things that are most precious, nothing is so excellent in it kind which may not be abused; so it is with this heavenly word: for it is and may be made a Charme two waies: First, when some part of it, is indeed used for a charm. Thus many Texts of Scripture, both in Latin and other languages, have been abused by Inchanters, as might easily be shewed. Secondly, when it is heard, read, recited, or made a matter of prayer without understanding. And thus the ignorant man, as much as in him lieth, makes it a Charme. For in his ordinary use thereof, he neither conceiveth nor taketh care to understand it, as lamentable experience teacheth. Yet in neither of these is the very bate repeating of the word effectuall. For as when a man heares or reades it, unlesse the Spirit of God enlighteneth his heart, it is to no purpose; so when it is made the matter of a Spell nothing will be effected, unlesse the devil either by confederacie, or superstitious conceit be drawne to conferre his help in the point, for his owne advantage. Howbeit, of all Inchantments these are the most dishonourable to God, most acceptable to Satan, and most hurtfull to the Charmer, which are made of the Scriptures. For beside the fiune of Witchcraft in the Charming, this inconvenience insueth, that Satan procureth more credit to one of these, then to twenty other, because the words are Scripture; hereby cloking his mischievous practises under the colour of holines, and so confirming the truth of that which the holy Ghost saith, that when he worketh most deceitfully, he transformes himselfe into an Angel of light, 2. Cor. 11. 14. He knoweth well, that ordinary words seeme nothing to some men, therefore he teacheth and suggesteth phrases and sentences out of the word, for such ungodly ends, that even the grace of them fetched from the Scriptures, may make them seeme powerfull. Wherefore let every one that is endued with grace and knowledge, duely consider this with himselfe. Cannot Gods word be effectuall, when it is used to edification, unlesse the worke of his own Spirit accompany the same? then surely it is impossible, that the same which is holy, beeing used to an evil end, should be powerfull, except the devil affoardeth his helpe for the effecting thereof. To conclude therefore, let men say what they will, the truth is this, that words of Inchantment, be they never so holy or prophane, either by way of cursing or blessing, have no power of themselves to the producing of strange workes; but are (as hath been said) onely diabolicall signes, admonishing the Devil of some wickednesse intended and desired, which he through his power must cause to be done. And thus much of Inchantment, standing upon the practise of wonders by a

Charme. To this head of Inchantment, sundry other practises of Witches are to be referred, the chiefe whereof are these. First, the using and making of Characters, Images, or Figures, specially the framing or Circles, for this ende to worke wonders by them. As to drawe the picture of a childe, or man, or other creature in clay or waxe, and to burie the same in the ground, or to hide it in some secret place, or to burne it in the fire, thereby intending to hurt or kill the party resembled. Againe, to make an impression into the said picture, by pricking or gashing the heart, or any other place with intent to procure dangerous or deadly paines to the same parts. This is a meere practise of Inchantment, and the making of the image, and using of it to this ende, is in vertue a Charme, though no words be used. For the bare picture hath no more power of it selfe to hurt the body reptesented, then bare words. All that is done commeth by the worke of the devil, who alone by the using of the picture in that sort is occasioned so or so, to worke the parties destruction. Secondly, hither we may referre the using of Amulets, that is, remedies and preservatives against in chantments, sorceries, and bewitchings, made of hearbes or some such things, and hanged about the pecke for that ende. Thirdly, the using of Exorcismes, that is, certaine set formes of words used in way of adjuration, for some extraordinary end. A practise usuall in the Church of Rome, whereby the Priest conjures the salt, holy water, creame, spittle, oyle, palmes, and c. all which are in truth meere inchantmets. For howsoever the Councell of Trent hath ratified them by their decrees, and so commended them to generall use within the compasse of the Popish Church; yet they have in them no power or ability of blessing or cursing, either by nature or Gods appointment. Fourthly, In this number we reckon the using of the name Jesus, to drive away the devil, or to prevent Witchcraft; a common practise among the ignorant. Wherein the wonderfull malice of Satan bewraies it selfe, in making the ignorant people think that Christ is a conjurer, and that there is vertue in the naming of his name, to doe some strange thing. Whereas the truth is, he careth neither for that name, nor for all the names of God, if a man goes no further then the bare repeating of them; but rather delighteth to see them so abused and disgraced. And hereupon it is, that in all conjurations, when he is raised by the Sorcerer, he is willing to be adjured by all the holy names of God that are in the Scripture, to the end that he may the more deepely seduce his owne in struments, and make them to thinke that these holy names will bind him, and force him to yield unto their desires in the particular, whe indeed there is no such matter. Which point throughly considered, may admonish us to take special heed of these cunning glozes and devillish insinuations, whereby he intendeth to delude us; alway remembring, that the Apostles themselves, to whom the power of working miracles was given, did never acknowledge the worke to be done by the name of Jesus, but as S. Peter affirmeth, through faith in his name, Act. 3. 6. 16. Fiftly, the crossing of the body, to this end, that we may be blessed from the devil. A thing usuall even of latter times, specially in Popery; wherein the crosse carrieth the very nature of a Charme, and the use of it in this manner, a practise of Inchantment. For God hath given no such vertue to a crosse, either by creation, or speciall privilege and appointment. Sixtly, the Scratching of a Witch to discover the Witch. For it is a meanes which hath no warrant or power thereunto, either by the word of God, or from nature, but onely from the Devil; who if he yieldeth either at crossing, or scratching, he doth it willingly, and not by compulsion, that he may feede his instrument with a false faith, and a superstitious conceit, to the dishonour of God, and their owne overthrow. In a word, looke whatsoever actions, gestures, signes, rites, and ceremonies are used by men or woman to worke wonders, having no power to effect the same, either by creation and nature, or by special appointment from God, they must all be referred to this head, and reckoned for Charmes. The Use. Now considering that all kinds of Charmes are the Devills watch words to cause him to worke the wonder, and have no vertue in them, be the words wherein they are conceived never so good: hereby we must be admonished, to take heede of the use of them, and all other unlawfull ceremonies, both in respect of their formes, be they praises or prayers, or imprecations; as also in regard of their ends, be they never so good in outward appearance. But alas the more lamentable is the case, Charming is in as great request as Physicke, and Charmes more sought unto, then Physitians in time of neede. There be charmes for all conditions and ages of men, for divers kinds of creatures, yea for every disease; as for head-ach, tooth-ach, stitches, and such like. Neverthelesse, howsoever some have subjected themselves to such base and ungodly meanes, yet the use hereof by the mercy of God, hath not been universall. And those that have sought for help, are to be advised in the feare of God, to repent of this their sinne, and to take a better course. Let them rightly consider, that they have hitherto depended upon Satan for helpe, and consequently have dishonored God, and renounced lawfull meanes sanctified by him, which should not have been done in case of the greatest worldly gain. For no man may do evil, that good may come of it. But they that use the helpe of Charmers, and consult with Wisemen, are wont to alledge something in decence or excuse of their practise. First, that they for their part, meane no hurt, they know no evil by the man whome they seeke to, they onely send to him, and he does them good, how and in what manner they regard not. Ans. 1. Indeed many be ignorant of the Inchanters courses. But in case of losse and hindrance, men ought not onely to inquire the meanes, but to waigh and consider the warrantablenes thereof; otherwise they doe not that they doe of faith, and so are guilty of sinne before God, Rom. 15. last v. 2. Put the case they themselves meane no hurt, yet in this action they doe hurt to themselves, by reposing trust in things, which upon better consideration they shall find to be dishonourable, and therefore hatefull to God. Secondly, they alledge; we goe to the Physitian for counsell, we take his Recipe, but we know not what it meaneth; yet, we use it, and find benefit by it; if this be lawfull, why may we not as well take benefit by the Wiseman, whose courses we be ignorant of? Ans. 1. Physicke used in time and place, is a worthy ordinance of God, and therefore beeing rightly used, God gives his blessing to it. But for Inchantment it was never sanctified by God, and therefore cannot be used in any assurance of his blessing. 2. The Physitians receit beeing a composition and mixture of natural things, though a man knowes it not, yet he takes it into his stomake, or applies it to his body, and sensibly perceives the vertue and efficacie thereof in the working: whereas the Charmers course consisteth of words, which neither are knowne in themselves, nor are manifest in their use to sense or understanding. And hereby it is plaine, there is not the same reason of Physicke and charmes: the one having a sensible operation by vertue given it of God; the other insensible, and wrought above ordinary meanes by the worke of Satan. Thirdly, they alleadge, God is mercifull, and he hath provided a salve for every sore; they have used other meanes, but they have not succeeded, and what should they doe more, may they not in extremity repaire to the Inchanter, and see what he can doe for them, rather then their goods and cattle should be lost and spoyled? Ans. 1. It were better for you to bide by the losse, yea to live and die in any sickenesse, then to tempt God by seeking helpe at charmers hands: for their helpe is dangerous, and commeth from the devil, whereupon if ye rest your selves, ye ioyne league with him, and so hazzard eternally the safetie both of bodies and soules. 2. Use good meanes allowed of God, and when they have beene used often without successe, proceed not to other courses, but referre your selves to God, and say with Job: The Lord hath given, and the Lord hath taken away; blessed be the name of the Lord, Job. 1. 21. And thus much of Inchanting, the first part of Operative Witchcraft. Sect. II. The second part is Jugling. Jugling is the deluding of the eye with some strange sleight done above the ordinary course of nature. In this description there are two points necessarily required in the point of Jugling, Delusion of the eye, and extraor dinarie

Sleight. Delusion is then performed, when a man is made to thinke he sees that which indeede he sees not. And this is done by operation of the devil diversely, but especially three waies. First, by corrupting the humor of the eye, which is the next instrument of sight. Secondly, by altering the ayre, which is the meane by which the object or species is carried to the eye. Thirdly, by altering and changing the object, that is, the thing seene, or whereon a man looketh. This deluding of the sense is noted by Paul, Gal. 3. 1. O foolish Galatians, who hath bewitched you? where the spirit of God useth a word borrowed from this kind of sorcerers, which in full meaning signifieth thus much: who hath deluded your eyes, and caused you to thinke you see that, which you see not. As if he should have said, Looke as the Jugler, by his devillish art, deludeth the out ward cie, and maketh men thinke they see that, which indeede they doe not: Even so the false Apostles, by their erroneous doctrine, have deluded the eyes of your mindes, and have caused you Galatians, to judge that to be the word of God, which is not, and that to be truth, which is errour and falshood. Paul gives us to understand by the very phrase used, that there is such a kind of Jugling, as is able to deceive the eye. For otherwise his comparison should not hold. The second thing required in Jugling, is a Sleight done above the order and course of nature. This is the point which maketh these cóveyances to be Witchcraft. For if they were within the compasse of nature, they could not be rightly tearmed and reputed Sorcerers: considering that divers men by reason of the agilitie of their bodies, and sleight of their hands, are able to worke divers seats, which seeme strange to the beholders, and yet not meddle with Witchcraft. Againe, some by the lawfull art of Opticks, may shew strange and admirable things, by meanes of light and darkenesse, and yet may be free from imputation of Magicall workes; because they keepe themselves wrioly within the power and practise of nature. But sleights done in Jugling over and above delusion, must passe the ordinary bounds and precincts of nature, and so are made points of Witchcraft. One memorable example, for the clearer manifestation of this point, we have in the Scripture, by name in the 7. 8. and 9. Chapters of Exodus, where Moses and Aaron, wrought wonders before Pharaoh, turning the rod into a serpent, and water into blood, with many other such like. Now Jannes and Jambres (for so Paul calleth them, 2. Tim. 3. 8.) the Magicians of Egypt, did worke the same miracles which Moses and Aaton had done: But here was the difference; Moses made true creatures, and wrought true miracles, whereas they did all in appearance and outward shewe. For theirs were not true reall actions, but onely Magicall illusions, wrought by the sleight and subtiltie of the devil, in the practise of Jugling. And because some thinke, that the serpents and frogs caused by the Magicians, were true creatures, and all their other workes as really and truly done as those which Moses and Aaron did, I will here stand a little to shew and proove the contrary, that they were onely in shew and appearance, and not in deed and truth. First then, if the frogs and serpents caused by Jannes and Jambres were true creatures indeede, and their other sleights true and reall workes; then they were made and caused either by the devil, or by God himselfe: (for no man of himselfe can make a rodde to become a true serpent.) But this was done neither by the devil, nor by God, as shall appeare in the sequele. They were not done by the Devil; because the devil cannot make a true creature, either serpent or frogge. How doth that appeare? Ans. To make a true creature of any sort, by producing the same out of the causes, is a worke serving to continue the creation, and is indeed a kinde of creation. Now the devil as he cannot create a thing at the first, so he is not able to continue the same by a new creation; that being a property belonging to God onely. For better conceiving hereof, we must knowe, that God createth two waies, either primarily in the beginning, when he made all things of nothing, Gen. 1. 1. or secondarily, in the government of the world, when he produceth a true creature in a true miracle; yet not making it of nothing (as he did in the beginning) but producing it by ministring and informing the matter immediately by himself, without the aide of ordinary meanes and instruments appointed after the creation. The former is creation properly called, the latter a continuance thereof. Both these God hath reserved to himselfe, as incommunicable to any creature. As for the succession and propagation of creatures in their kinds, as of men, beasts, birds, fishes, and c. it is onely a continuation of the creatures in their kinds, and is wrought by ordinary meanes of generation; but is no continuance of the worke of the creation. And the devil by his power may make counterfeits of the true creatures of God, but neither by creating them, not by continuing their creation; these two beeing workes peculiar and proper to the Deity alone. Againe, if the devil could turne a rodde into a true serpent, and water into blood indeed, then his power should be equall to the power of the Sonne of God himselfe. For the first miracle that he wrought, was the turning of water into wine, Joh. 2. And that was no greater a worke, then the turning of water into bloode, or a rodde into a serpent. But this were most horrible blasphemie, to match the devil with the Sonne of God, and his finite power, with the power of the Godhead, by which miracles are wrought. And the truth is, Satan can worke no true miracles: neither doth the text import, that the Magicians did that which they did by miracle, but by Inchantment and Sorcery, Exod. 7.11.22.and 8.7. In the second place, I affirme that God did not create these creatures, or cause the workes of the Magicians to be effected. And this is prooved by the words of Paul, 2. Tim. 3. 8. who saith that Jannes and Jambres (which did these workes) withstood Moses and Aron, whom God had sent, and by whó he wrought. If then God had wrought with the Magicians also, he should have been against himselfe, yea, he should have wrought both wayes, for himselfe, and against himselfe, and consequently should have impeached his owne glorie, for the manifestation whereof he wrought miracles by Moses and Aron; which we may not once think of God. Seeing therefore that these serpents, if they were true creatures, were not created either by Satan, because he could not, or by God himselfe, because he would not; it must needs remaine, that they, and all other the Magicians workes, were meere illusions, and not otherwise. Yet for the further clearing of the matter in hand: the text it selfe yieldeth sundry reasons, to proove that these acts of the Sorcerers, were but appearances, and not things really produced. First, they that cannot doe a lesser thing, can not possibly do a greater. Now Moses sheweth that the Egyptian Inchanters could not doe a lesser thing, then the turning of roddes into true serpents, or waters into blood. For they could not by all their power and skill, preserve themselves from the plagues of Egypt, as the botch, and other indgements, Exod. 9. 11. which was a more easie thing, then to make or change a creature. Nay, they were not able to bring forth lice by their Inchantment, which seemeth to be the least miracle, but acknowledged that to be the finger of God, Exod. 8. 18, 19. Secondly, the text saith, that Aarons serpent devoured their serpents, Exod. 7. 12. hence it follows, that theirs could not be true creatures. For in all likelihood they were all of the same kind, and of like quantity, at least in shew. And it was never seene, that one creature should receive into it selfe an other creature of equall bignes, with preservation of it selfe. Neither hath it been observed ordinarily, that one creature should devoure another of the same kind. It was therefore a work of Gods secret power in the true serpent, whereby he would shew that the other were not true and reall, but formall and imaginary. Thirdly, if the Magicians had been able to have made true frogges and serpents, then by the same power they might have remooved those which Moses brought; for the like ability is required in both: yet this they could not do, but were faine to intreat Moses, to pray for their remoovall. So saith the text, Then Pharaoh called for Moses and Aaron, and said, Pray, and c. Exod. 8.8. Lastly, the frogges which Moses caused, when they were remooved, beeing gathered on heapes, caused great corruption, and the whole land stanke of them, Exod.8. 14. Againe, the water turned into blood, made the fish in the river to die, and the water to stinke, so that the Egyptians could not drinke of the water of the river, Exod. 7. 21. But we read of no such effect of the frogges and waters of the Inchanters, which doubtlesse would have followed as well as the other, if both had been true and reall creatures. It remaines therefore, that these were but meere appearances and Jugling tricks, and the Sorcerers themselves Juglers, yea all their works but sleights, caused by the power and subtilty of Satan, and no true workes, as hath been said. Thus I have declared the whole nature, grounds, and kinds of this damnable Art.

CHAP. V.

What Witches be, and of how many sorts.

HAving in the former part of this Treatise opened the nature of Witchcraft, and ther by made way for the better understanding of this Judiciall Law of Moses, I come now to shew who is the practiser hereof, whome the Text principally aimeth at, namely, the Witch, whether man or woman. A Witch is a Magician, who either by open or secret league, wittingly, and willingly, consenteth to use the aide and assistance of the Devil, in the working of Wonders. First, I call the Witch [a Magician] to shew what kind of person this is: to wit, such a one as doth professe and practise Witchcraft. For a Magician is a professor and a practiser of this art, as may appeare, Act. 8. 9. where Simon a Witch of Samaria is called Magus, or Simon the Magician. Againe, in this generall tearme, I comprehend both sexes or kinds of persons, men and women, excluding neither from beeing Witches. A point the rather to be remembred, because Moses in this place setting down a Judiciall Law against Witches, useth a word of the feminine gender [mecashephab] which in English properly signifieth, a woman Witch: whereupon some might gather, that women onely were Witches. Howbeit Moses in this word exempteth not the male, but onely useth a notion referring to the semale, for good causes; principally for these two. First, to give us to understand, that the woman beeing the weaker sexe, is sooner intangled by the devils illusions with this damnable art, then the man. And in all ages it is found true by experience, that the devil hath more easily and oftener prevailed with women, then with men. Hence it was, that the Hebrewes of ancient times, used it for a proverb, The more women, the more Witches. His first temptation in the beginning, was with Eve a woman, and since he pursueth his practise accordingly, as making most for his advantage. For where he findeth easiest entrance, and best entertainment, thither will he oftnest resort. Secondly, to take away all exception of punishment from any party that shall practise this trade, and to shew that weakenesse cannot exempt the Witch from death. For in all reason, if any might alledge infirmity, and plead for favour, it were the womá, who is weaker then the man, But the Lord saith, if any person of either sexe among his people, be found to have entred covenant with Satan, and become a practiser of Sorcery, though it be a woman and the weaker vessell, she shall not escape, she shall not be suffred to live, she must die the death. And thogh weaknes in other cases, may lessen both the crime and the punishment, yet in this it shall take no place. The second point in the description, is consenti touse the helpe of the devil, either by open or secret league, wittingly and willingly: wherein standeth the very thing, that maketh a Witch to be a Witch: The yielding of consent upon covenant. By which clause, two sort of people are expressely excluded from beeing Witches, First, such as be tainted with phrenzy or madnesse, or are through weaknesse of the braine deluded by the devil. For these, though they may be said after a sort to have society with Satan, or rather he with them, yet they cannot give their consent to use his aide truly, but onely in imagination; with the true Witch it is farre otherwise. Secondly, all such superstitious persons, men or women, as use Charmes and Inchantment for the effecting of any thing upon a superstitious and erroneous perswasion, that the Charmes have vertue in them to doe such things, not knowing that it is the action of the devil by those meanes; but thinking that God hath put vertue into them, as he hath done into herbes for Physicke. Of such persons we have (no doubt) abundance in this our Land, who though they deale wickedly, and sinne grievously in using Charmes, yet because they intend not to joyne league with the devil, either secretly, or formally, they are not to be counted Witches. Nevertheless, they are to be advertised in the meane time, that their estate is fearefull. For their present ungodly practices have prepared the already to this cursed trade, and may bring them in time to be the ranekest Witches that can be. Wherefore I advise all ignorant persons, that know not God not the Scriptures, to take heed and beware of this dangerous evil, the use of Charmes. For if they be once convinced in their consciences, and know that God hath given no power to such means, and yet shall use them, assuredly they doe in effect consent to the devil to be helped by him, and thereupon are joyned in confederacy with him in the confidence of their vine hearts, and so are become Witches. The third and last thing in the description is the end of Witchcraft; The working of wonders. Wonders are wrought three wayes (on hath beene shewed,) either by Divination, or by enchantment, or by Jugling: and to one of obese three heads all feates and practices of Withcraft are to be referred. Now if any man doubt; whether these be such Witches indeed as have been described let him remember, that besides experience in all ages and countries, we have also sundry examples of them even in Scriptures. In the old Testament we reade of Baiaam, Num. 23. who though he be called a Prophet, because he was so reputed of men, yet indeed he was a notorious Witch, both by profession and practise, and would have shewed his cunning in that kind upon the Israelites, if God had not hindered him against his will. Of the same kind were the Inchanters of Egypt Exod, 7. the Witches of Persia, Dan. 2. and the Pythonisse of Endor, knowne for a renowned Sorcerer over all Israel:and therefore Sauls servants being asked, could presently tel of her, as we read, Sam. 28. In the new Testament, mention is made of Simon, whose name declared his prosession; his name was Magus; and the text saith, that he used Witchcraft, and bewitched the people of Samaria, calling himselfe a great man; Act. 8. 9. Whence it was that after his death, there was a statue set up in Rome in honour of him in the daies of Claudius Cæsar, with this inscription; Simoni Deo Sancto. And it is not unlike, but Bar-iesus the false Prophet at Paphus, was a man addicted to the practices of Witchcraft, and for that cause was called by a kind of excellencie, Elymas the Magician, Act. 13. 6.8. that is, the great or famous

Sorcerer. Lastly, the Pythonisse at Philippi, that gather master much advantage by divining Act. 16. 16. And all these used the helpe of the devil, for the working of wonders. Of Witches there be two sorts: The had Witch, and the good Witch: for so they are commonly called.

The bad Witch, is he or she that hath consented in league with the devil to use his helpe, for the doing of hurt only as to strike and annoy the bodies of men, women, children, and cattle with diseases, and with death it selfe: so likewise to raise tempests, by sea and by land, and c. This is commonly called the binding Witch. The good Witch, is he or shee that by consent in a league with the devil, doth use his help for the doing of good onely. This cannot hurt, torment, curse or kill, but onely heale and cure the hurts inflicted upon men or cattle, by bad Witches. For as they can doe no good, but onely hurt:so this can doe no hurt, but good only. And this is that order which the devil hath set in his kingdom, appointing to severall persons their severall offices and charges. And the good Witch is commonly tearmed the unbinding Witch. Now how soever both these be evil, yet of the two, the more horrible and detestable Monster is the good Witch: for looke in what place soever there be bad Witches that hurt onely, there also the devil hath his good ones, who are better knowne then the bad, beeing commonly called Wisemen, or Wisewoman. This will appeare by experiéce in most places in this country. For let a mans child, friend, or cattle be taken with some fore sickenesse, or strangely tormented with some rare and unknowne disease, the first thing he doth, is to bethinke himselfe and inquire after some Wiseman or Wisewoman, and thither he sends and goes for helpe. When he comes, he first tells them the flare of the sicke man: the Witch then beeing certified of the disease, prescribeth either Charmes of words to be used over him, or other such counterfeit meanes, wherein there is no vertue; beeing nothing else but the Devils Sacraments, to cause him to doe the cure, if it come by Witchcraft. Well, the meanes are received, applyed, and used, the sicke party accordingly recovereth, and the conclusion of all is, the usual acclamation; Oh happie is the day, that ever I met with such a man or woman to helpe me! Here observe, that both have a stroke in this action:the bad Witch hurt him, the good healed him; but the truth is, the latter hath done him a thousand times more harme then the former. For the one did only hurt the body, but the devil by meanes of the other, though he have left the body in good plight, yet he hath laid fast hold on the soule, and by curing the body, hath killed that. And the party thus cured, cannot say with David, The Lord is my helper; but the devil is my helper; for by him he is cured. Of both these kindes of Witches the present Law of Moses must be understood. This point well considered, yieldeth matter both of instruction and practise. Of instruction, in that it shewes the cunning and crafty dealing of Satan, who afflicteth and tormenteth the body for the gaine of the foule. And for that purpose hath so ordered his instruments, that the bad Witch gives the occasion, by annoying the bodie or goods; and the good immediately accomplisheth his desire, by intangling the soule in the bands of errour, ignorance, and false faith. Againe, this sheweth the blindnesse of naturall corruption, specially in ignorant and superstitious people. It is their nature to abhorred hurtfull persons, such as bad Witches be, and to count them execrable; but those that doe them good, they honour and reverence as wife men and women, yea, seeke and sue unto them in times of extremitie, though of al persons in the world, they be most odious: and Satan in them seemes the greatest friend, when he is most like himselfe, and intendeth greatest mischiefe. Let all ignorant persons be advised here of in time, to take heed to themselves, and learne to knowe God and his word, that by light from thence they may better discerne of the subtill practises of Satan and his instruments. For matter of practise; Hence we learne our dutie, to abhorre the Wizzard, as the most pernicious enemie of our salvation, the most effectuall instrument of destroying our soules, and of building up the devils kingdome: yea, as the greatest enemie to Gods name, worship, and glorie, that is in the world next to Sathan himselfe. Of this fort was Simon Magus, who by doing strange cures and workes, made the people of Samaria to take him for some great man, who wrought by the mighty power of God, whereas he did all by the devil. He therefore beeing a good Witch, did more hurt in seducing the people of God, then Balaam a bad one could with all his curses. And we must remember that the Lord hath set a lawe upon the Witches head, he must not live, and if death be due to any, then a thousand deaths of right belong to the good Witch. But the patrons of Witches endeavour to delude the true interpretation of the Law. For by a Witch (lay they) we must understand a poisoner, and they alledge for that purpose the 70. Interpreters, who translate the originall word [Mecashephab] by which signifieth a poisoner. I answer: First, the word used by the 70. Interpreters signifieth indeed so much, yet not that onely, but also a Witch in generall, as may appeare in sundry places of Scripture. The Apostle, reckoning up Witchcraft among the workes of the slesh, useth the Greeke word , not for poisoning, but for al Magical arts, as Hierome testifieth upon the place. And that it must necessarily be so translated, it is evident, because in the next verse murther is termed another worke of the flesh, under which, poisoning and all other kinds of killing are comprehended: And the same word is used in the like sense, Reu. 21. 8. and 22. 15. Againe, the word [Mecashephah] which Moses useth, is ascribed to the Inchanters of Egypt, in the 7. 8. and 9. chapters of Exodus; and to the wisemen of Babel, Dan. 2. who are also called in the translation of the Seventie: and both sorts of them were Witches and Sorcerers. The kings of Egypt and Babylon used these [Mecashephim] for sundrie purposes, and made them of their counsell; and if they had bin according to this allegatió, poisoners; it is not like they would have so fitted the humors of those two Princes, Pharaoh and Nebuchadnetsar, much lesse that they would have so ordinarily required their presence and assistance, in the busines there mentioned. Thirdly, there is a peremptorie Law against the willfull murtherer, Num. 35. 31. that he should be put to death, and that no recompense should be taken for his life. In which place all poisoners are condemned, because they are wilfull murtherers. Now if here in Exodus, by [Mecashephah] we should understand a poisoner, then there should be one and the same law twice propounded for the same thing, which is not like: and therefore the word used by Moses in this text, signifieth not a poisoner properly, but a Witch.

CHAP. VI.

Of the punishment of Witches.

HItherto I have treated of the nature of Witchcraft, both in generall, and particular, and have also shewed what Witches are, both good and badde. And now I proceede to the second point considered in this Text, the Punishment of a Witch, and that is Death. In the Judiciall lawes of Moles (wherof this is one) the Lord appointed sundry penalties, which in qualities and degree differed one from another, so as according to the nature of the offence, was the proportion and measure of the punishment ordained. And of al sinnes, as those were the most heinous in account, which tended directly to the dishonour of God, so to them was assigned death, the greatest and highest degree of punishment. He that despised the Law of Moses, died without mercie under two or three witnesses, Hebr. 10. 28. the punishment of the these, was restitution fourefold, Exod, 22. 1. but the murtherer must be put to death, Num. 35. 31. the Idolater and Seducer were commanded to be slaine, Exod. 22. 20. Deut. 13. 5. the Blasphemer must be stoned, Leuit. 29. 19. And the Witch is numbred amongst these grievous offenders; therefore his punishment is as great as any other. For the text saith, he might not be suffered to live, Exod. 22. 18. But why should the Witch be so sharply censured? And what should moove the Lord to allot so high a degree of punishment to that sort of offenders? Ans. The cause was not the hurt, which they brought upon men in body, goods, or outward estate. For there be sundry that never did harme, but good only. We read not of any great hurt that was done by the Inchanters of Egypt, or by the Pythonisse of Endor, or by Simon Magus in Samaria. And those divining witches, which have taken upon them to foretell things to come, hurt not any, but themselves, yet they must die the death. This therefore is not the cause. But what if these doe hurt, or kill, must they not then die? yes verily, but by another law, the lawe of murther, and not by the law of Witchcraft: For in this case, he dieth as a murtherer, and not as a Witch, and so he should die, though he were no Witch. The cause then of this sharpe punishment, is the very making of a league with the Devil, either secret, or open, whereby they covenant to use his helpe for the working of wonders. For by vertue of this alone it commeth to passe, that Witches can doe strange things, in Divining, Inchanting, and Jugling. Now let it be observed, of what horrible impietie they stand guiltie before God, who joynd in confederacie with Satan. Hereby they renounce the Lord that made them, they make no more account of his savior and protection, they doe quite cut themselves off from the covenant made with him in Baptisme, from the communion of the Saints, from the true worship and service of God. And on the contrary they give themselves unto Satan, as their godly whome they continually feare and serve. Thus are they become the most detestable enemies to God, and his people, that can be. For this cause Samuel told Saul, that rebellion was as the sin of Witchcraft: that is, a most heinous and detestable sinne in the sight of God. The traytour, that doth no hurt to his neighbour, but is willing and readie to doe him the best service that can be desired, is not with standing by the law of Nations, no better then a dead man, because he betraies his Soveraigne and consequently can not be a friend unto the Common-wealth. In like manner, though the Witch were in many respects profitable, and did no hurt, but procured much good; yet because he hath renounced God his king and governour, and hath bound himselfe by other lawes to the service of the enemy of God and his Church, death is his portion justly assigned him by God; he may not live.

CHAP. VII.

The application of the do doctrine of Wiechcraft to our simes.

THus having delivered the true sense and interpretation of this Judiciall Law, both concerning the sinne of Witchcraft, and the persons, by whome this sinne is practised; it remaineth now that I should make some use thereof, by way of application to the Witches of our times. In doing whereof, foure particular Questions of moment, are to be handled. I. Whether the Witches of our times, be the same with those, that are here condemned by the lawe of Moses? for some there be, and those men of learning, and members of Gods Church, that holde they are not. II. If they be the same (as it shall appeare they are) then how we may in these daies be able to discerne, and discover a Witch? III. What Remedie may be used against the hurt of Witchcraft? IV. Whether our Witches are to be punished with death, and that by vertue of this lawe of Moses? Sect. I. I. Question. Whether the Witches of our times, be the same with those that are here condemned by Moses Laws. Ans. If we doe well consider the qualitie, and condition of the Witches of our daies, we shall easily see, that they be the same. For experience sheweth, that whether they be men or women, but especially aged women, they be such persons, as doe renounce God, and their Baptisime, and make a league with the devil, either secretly or openly; in which the devil bindeth himselfe to teach them certaine rites and cesemonies, whereby they may be able to worke wonders, or to stirre up tempests, to reveal secrets, to kill or hurt men, and cattle, or to cure and doe good, according to the tenour of these couchant. The confessions of Witches recorded in the Chronicles of countries through all Europe, doe with condition consent declare and manifest this point. So that how soever our Witches may differ in some circumstances fró those in the time of Moses, as either in the instrument, and moans used, or in the manner and forme, or in some particular ends of their pracli sess yet in the substance and foundation of Witchcraft, they agree with them. For both of them have made a convenant with the Devil one way or other, and by vertue thereof have wrought wonders above the order of nature. Agreeing therefore in the very foundation, and forme of Witchcraft, which is the league, and in the proper end, the working of wonders: they must needes be in substance and effect the same with the Witches mentioned by Moses. And yet this point is denied by some, and the Witches of these daies have their patrons, who use reasons to proove that now we have none such as we speak of. Their reasós are specially three. First, they labour to take away the forme of Witchcraft, affirming that there can be no confederacie made betweene the Witch and the Devil, and that for foure causes. I. In every league and contract, the parties must be mutually bound each to other: now betweene man or woman and the Devil, there can be no bond made, and though there could, yet man is bound in conscience to God, to renounce the bond of obedience to Satan, and to breake the covenant. Ans. There be two sorts of leagues; lawfull, and unlawfull: in all lawfull leagues it is true, that there must be a mutuall bond of both parties each to other, which may not be dissolved; but in unlawfull compacts it is otherwise. And no man can say that this league betweene a Witch and the Devil is lawfull, but wicked and damnable; yet beeing once made, howsoever unlawfully, it is a league and compact. This therefore prooveth not, that there can be no covenant at all, but that there can be no lawfull covenant betwixt them, which no man will deny. II. Satan and the Witch are of divers natures: he is spiritual, they are corporall substances: therefore there can be no league made betweene them. Ans. The reason is not good. For even God himselfe, who is of nature most simple and spirituall, made a covenant with Adam, renued the same unto Abraham, Isaac, and Jacob: and continued it with his Church on earth, from age to age. Hence is appeareth, that diversitie of nature in the parties, cannot hinder the making of a covenant. And therefore if man may make covenant with God himselfe, who is most spirituall; then may he likewise come in league with the Devil, whose substance is not so pure and spirituall. Againe, we must remember, that in making of a covenant, it is sufficient, that the parties consent and agree in will and understanding, though other circumstances and rites, which are but signes of confirmation, be wanting. Be it then, that Satá hath not a bodily substance, as man hath, yet considering that man is indued with understanding, to conceive of things, as the devil doth, and hath also will to yield consent, and approbation thereunto, though in a corrupt and wicked manner, there may passe a confederacie, and a covenant may be made, and stand in sorce betweene them. III. Whatsoever the devil doth in this compact, he doth it in fraud and deceit, never meaning in his promises, as man doth: and when both parties meane not one and the same thing, how can they grow to agreement in any kind? Ans. Suppose this be true, yet it onely prooveth, that the covenant made between them, was deceitfull, and unlawfull. But what of that? still it remaineth a bargain howsoever: for it faileth only in the circumstance, the substance, which is the consent of the parties, was not wanting. IV. Witches of our times (say they) are aged persons, of weake braines, and troubled with abundance of melancholie, and the devil taketh advantage of the humor, and so deludes them, perswading that they have made a league with him, when they have not, and consequently mooving them to imagine that they doe, and may do strange things, which indeed are done by himselfe, and not by them. Ans. This reason is a meere melancholike conceit, without ground. And the contrary is a manifest truth, that they are not so, as is affirmed, parties deceived by reasó of their humors. For first, our Witches are as wise and politike, yea as crafty and cunning in all other matters, as other men be; whereas brainsicke persons troubled with melancholy, if their undetstanding be distempered in one action, it will be faultie likewise in others more or lesse. Againe, our Witches know that they sinne in the practises of Witchcraft, and therefore they use subtile meanes to cover them; and hee that would convict them, must have great dexterity to goe beyond them. Now if they were persons deluded, through corruption of any humours; looke what humour caused them to do a thing, the same would urge them to disclose it. Thirdly, they are also of the same stamp, they take the same courses in all their practises; their consent in word and action is uniuersall. Men of learning have observed, that all Witches through Europe, are of like carriage and behaviour, in their examinations and convictions; they use the same answers, refuges, defenses, protestations. In a word, looke what be the practises and courses of the Witches in England, in any of these particulars, the same be the practises of the Witches in Spaine, France, Italy, Germany, and c. Wherefore the case is cleare, they are not deluded by Sathan, through the force of humor, as is avouched; for such persons, accordingly as they are diversly taken, would shew themselves diversly affected, and varie in their speeches, actions, and conceipts, both publike and private. Fourthly, our Witches are wont to communicate their skill to others by tradition, to teach and instruct their children and posterity, and to initiate them in the grounds, and practises of their owne trade, while they live, as may appeare by the confessions recorded in the courts of all countries. But if they were persons troubled with melancholie, their conceipts would die with them. For conceits, and imaginarie fancies, which rise of any humor, cannot be conveyed from partie to party, no more then the humor it selfe. Lastly, if this slight might serve to defend Witches under pretence of delusion thorough corrupted humours, then here were a cover for all manner of sinnes. For example: a fellon is apprehended for robberie or murther, and is brought before the judge: Upon examination he confesseth the fact, beeing convicted, the láw proceeds to condemnation. The same mans friends come in and alleadge before the Judge in this máner; This man hath a crazie braine, and is troubled with melancholy, and though he hath confessed the fact, yet the truth is, it was not he, but the devil who himselfe committed the murther, and made him thinke he did it, when he did it not, and hereupon he hath confessed. Would any man thinke that this were a reasonable allegation, and a sufficient meane to moove the Judge to acquit him? Assuredly if it were, upon the same ground might any sinne be laid upon the devils backe, and all good lawes and judiciall proceedings be made voide. Therefore howsoever the patrons of Witches be learned men, yet they are greatly deceived in fathering the practises of Sorcery upon a melancholy humour. But for the further ratifying of their assertion, they proceede, and use this argument: They which confesse of them selves things false and impossible, must needes be parties deluded: but our Witches doe this, when they be examined or consulted with; as that they can raise tempests, that they are carried through the aire in a moment, from place to place, that they passe through key-holes, and clifts of doores, that they be sometimes turned into cats, hares, and other creatures; lastly, that they are brought into farre countries, to meete with Herodias, Diana, and the Devil, and such like; all which are meere fables, and things impossible. Answ. We must make a difference of Witches in regard of time. There is a time, when they first begin to make a league with Satan, and a time also after the league is made and confirmed. When they first beginne to grow in confederacies with the devil, they are sober, and their understanding sound, they make their match waking, and as they thinke wisely enough, knowing both what they promise the Devil, and upon what conditions, and therefore all the while it is no delusion. But after they be once in the league, and have been intangled in compact with the devil (considerately as they thinke, for their own good and advantage) the case may be otherwise. For then reason and understanding may be depraved, memorie weakned, and all the powers of their soule blemished. Thus becomming his vassals, they are deluded, and so intoxicated by him, that they will run into thousands of fantastical imaginations, holding themselves to be transformed into the shapes of other creatures, to be transported in the ayre into other countries, yea to doe many strange things, which in truth they doe not. I come now to their second reason. The Witches of our age (say they) were not known in the dayes of Moses, nor of Christ, therefore the law concerneth them not. To this I answer two wayes: First, that their argument is naught: for by the same reason the Papists might avouch the lawfulnes of the images of Saints, as of Peter, Paul, and others, yea of Christ himselfe, because they were not knowne in the daies of Moses, and therefore could not be condemned in the second Commandment. Whereas contrarily, the spirit of God, hath so framed and penned the lawes Morall, and Judiciall, which concerne man, as that they fetch within their compasse all sinnes of all ages, and condemne them. And therefore whatsoever is against the Lawe of God written by Moses, though it were not knowne, nor heard of, either when the law was made, or afterward, is yet condemned by the same Law. Againe, I answer, that our Witches are the same that were in Moses time: and therefore by their owne reason must needes be condemned by this Judiciall law. For by the records of ancient writers it is proofed, that about a 1200. years before Christs birth, shortly after the Troian warre, which was 100. yeare and upward before the building of the Temple by Salomon, there were the same Witches that are now, as the Circes and Syrenes, and such like mentioned in the narration of that warre, as is manifest to them that know the story. Againe, 500. yeares before Christ, when the Romans made their twelve Tables, which comprised all the lawes whereby that famous Commonwealth was governed, they made one expressely against Witches, even the same with these of our time, for practising the same things, as blasting of corne, hurting of cattle, men, women, and children, and c. And for the time of Christ, though there be no particular mention made of any such Witches; yet thence it followeth not, that there were none: for all things that then happened, were not recorded: and I would faine know of the chiefe patrós of them, whether those parties possessed with the devil, and troubled with strange diseases, whome Christ healed, and out of whom he casts devils, were not bewitched with some such people, as our Witches are? if they say no, let them if they can proove the contrary. The third and last reason is this: Christ at his comming abolished all sinne, and therefore miracles and Witchcraft then ceased also. The Apostle saith, that hee spoiled principalities and powers, and triumphed over them upon the crosse, Col. 2.15. Ans. This argument is frivolous, serving as well to justisie the traytor, the theese, and the murtherer, as the witch. For whereas it is alledged, that Christ abolished all sinne: we must understand how? not simply, so as sinne should be no more, but onely in part, in this life, reserving the finall destruction thereof to the last judgement. Againe, sinne is not abolished, no not in part unto all, but onely to the members of Christ. Whereupon the Apostle saith, There is no condemnation to them that are in Christ, Rom. 8.1. because no sinne is imputed unto them. But unto Witches, and all the enemies of Christ, sinne is imputed, and not abolished. To conclude, howsoever much is said in their deféce, yet the first part is cleare affirmatively, that the Witches of our time, are the same with the witches that were in Moses time, in truth and substance. And so much for the first Question. Sect. II. II. Quest. How we may bee able in these our daies to discerne, and discover a Witch. Ans. The discoverie of a Witch is a matter Judiciall, as is also the discoverie of a these and a murtherer, and belongeth not to every man, but is to be done Judicially by the Magistrate, according to the forme and order of Law; who therefore is set a part for such ends, and hath authority both to discover, and punish the enemies of God and his Church. Now for the Magistrates direction in this busines, we are to knowe, that in the discovery of a Witch, two things are required, Examination, and Conviction. § 1. Examination is an action of the Magistrate, making speciall enquirie of the crime of Witchcraft. This action must have the beginning from occasions, and presumptions. For the Magistrate though he be a publike person, and stand in the roome of God, for the execution of Justice, yet he may not take UPON him to examine whome and how himselfe willeth of any crime; neither ought he to proceede upon sleight causes, as to shew his authority over others, or UP sinister respects, as to revenge his malice, or to bring parties into danger or suspition; but he must proceed upon speciall presumptions. Those I call presumptions, which do at least probably, and conjecturally note one to be a Witch; and these are certaine signes, whereby the party may be discovered: I will touch some few of them. The first in order is this: If any person, man, or woman, be notoriously defamed for such a party. Notorious defamation, is a common report of the greater sort of people, with whom the partie suspected dwelleth, that he or she is a Witch. This yieldeth a strong suspition. Yet the Magistrate must be warie in receiving such a report. For it falls out oftentimes, that the innocent may be suspected, and some of the better sort notoriously defamed. Therefore the wise and prudent Judge ought carefully to looke, that the report be made by men of honesty and credit: which if it be, he may then proceed to make further enquirie of the fact. The second is, if a fellow-witch or Magician give testimonie of any person to be a Witch, either voluntarily, or at his or her examinatió, or at his or her death. This is not sufficient for conviction, or condemnation, but onely a fit presumption to cause strait examination of the party to be made. Thirdly, if after cursing, there followeth death, or at least some mischeiefe. For Witches are wont to practise their mischievous facts by cursing and banning. This also is a sufficient matter of Examination, not of Conviction. Fourthly, if after enmitie, quarrelling, or threatning, a preset mischiefe doth follow. For parties devilishly disposed, after cursings do use threatnings; and that also is a great presumption Fiftly, if the party suspected be the sonne or daughter, the manservant or maidservant, the familiar friend, neere neighbour, or old companion of a knowne and convicted Witch. This may be likewise a presumption. For Witchcraft is an art that may be learned, and conveyed from man to man, and often it falleth out, that a Witch dying

108

leaveth some of the forenamed, heires of her Witchcraft. Sixtly, some do adde this for a presumption; If the party suspected be found to have the devils marke: for it is commonly thought, when the devil maketh his covenant with them, he alwaies leaveth his marke behind him, whereby be knowes them for his owne. Now if by some casuall meanes, such a marke be descried on the body of the party suspected, whereof no evident reason in nature can be given, the Magistrate in this case may cause such to be examined, or take the matter into his owne hand, that the truth may appeare. Lastly, if the party examined be unconstant, or contrary to himselfe in his deliberate answers, it argueth a guilty minde and conscience which stoppeth the freedome of speech and utterance, and may give just occasion to the Magistrate to make further inquirie. I say not if he or she be timorous and fearefull: for a good man may be fearefull in a good cause, sometimes by nature, sometime in regard of the presence of the Judge, and the greatness of the audience. Againe some may be soddenly taken, and others naturally want the liberty of speech, which other men have. And these are the causes of feare and astonishment, which may befall the good, as well as the bad. Touching the manner of Examination, there be two kinds of proceeding; either by a single Question, or by some Torture. A single question is, when the magistrate himself only maketh enquirie what was done, or not done, by bare and naked interrogations. A torture is, when besides the enquiry in words, he useth also the racke, or some other violent meanes to urge confession. This course hath been taken in some countries, and may no doubt lawfully and with good conscience be used, howbeit not in every case, but only upon strong and great presumptions going before, and when the party is obstinate. And thus much for Examination: now followeth Conviction. § 2. Conviction, is an action of the Magistrate, after just examination, discovering the Witch. This action must proceed from just and sufficient proofes, and not from bare presumptions. For though presumptions give occasion to examine, yet they are no sufficient causes of conviction. Now in generall the proofes used for conviction are of two sorts, some be lesse sufficient, some be more sufficient. The lesse sufficient proofes are these. First, in former ages, the party suspected of Witchcraft, was brought before the Magistrate, who caused red hoat iron, and scalding water to be brought, and commanded the party to put his hand in the one, or to take up the other, or both, and if he took up the iron in his bare hand without burning, or endured the water without scalding, hereby he was cleared, and judge free: but if he did burne or scalde, he was then convicted, and condemned for a Witch. But this manner of conviction, hath long agone been condemned for wicked and diabolicall, as in truth it is, considering that thereby many times, an innocent man may be condemned, and a rancke Witch scape unpunished. Againe, out owne times have afforded instances of such weake and insufficient proofes. As first, Scratching of the suspected party, and present recovery thereupon. Secondly, burning of the thing bewitched, if it be not a man, as a hogge, or oxe, or such like creature, is imagined to be a forcible meanes to cause the Witch to discover herself. Thirdly, the burning of the thatch of the suspected parties house, which is thought to bee able to cure the party bewitched, and to make the Witch to betray her selfe. Besides these, in other countries they have a further proofe justified by some that be learned. The party is taken, and bound hand and foot, and cast crosse waies into the water, if she sinke, she is counted innocent, she escapeth, if she fleete on the water, and sincke not, she is taken for a Witch, conuicted, and accordingly punished. All these proofes are so farre from being sufficient, that some of them, if not all, are after a sort practises of Witchcraft, having in them no power or vertue to detect a Sorcerer, either by Gods ordinance in the creation, or by any speciall appointment since. For what vertue can the Scratching of a Witch have to cure a hurt? where doe we finde it in any part of the word of God, that scratching should be used? or what promise of recovery upon the use thereof. But how then comes it to passe, that helpe is often procured by these and such like means? Ans. It is the sleight and subtiltie of the devil upon scratching the Witch, to remove such hurts, as himselfe hath inflicted, that thereby he may inure men to the practise of wicked and superstitious meanes. And what I say of scratching, the same may be enlarged to all other proofes of this kind before named: God hath imprinted no such vertue in their natures to these purposes, or added the same unto them by speciall and extraordinary assignment. That therefore which is brought to passe by them when they are used, commeth from the devil. And yet to justifie the casting of a Witch into the water, it is alledged, that having made a covenant with the devil, she hath renounced her Baptisms, and hereupon their growes an Antipathie, betweene her and water. Answ. This allegation serves to no purpose: for all water is not the water of Baptisme, but that only which is used in the very act of Baptisme, and not before nor after. The element out of the use of the Sacrament, is no Sacrament, but returnes againe to his common use. To goe yet further, an other insufficient proofe, is the testimonie of some wizzard. It hath been the ordinary custome of some men, when they have had any thing ill at ease, presently to goe or send to some wise man, or wise woman, by whom they have been informed, that the thing is bewitched; and to winne credit to their answer, some of them have offered to shewe the Witches face in a glasse: whereof the party having taken notice, returnes home, and detested the man or woman of Witchcraft. This I grant may be a good presumption to cause strait examination: but a sufficient proofe of conviction it cannot be. For put the case the grand-Jurie at the Assises goeth on a party suspected, and in their consultation the Devil comes in the likenesse of some knowne man, and tells them the person in question is indeed a Witch, and offers withall to confirme the same by other; should the Inquest receive his other or accusation to condemne the man? Assuredly no; and yet that is as much as the testimonie of another wizzard, who onely by the devils holpe revealeth the

Witch. If this should be taken for a sufficient proofe, the devil would not leave one good man alive in the world. Againe, all other presumptions commonly used, are insufficient, though they may minister occasion of triall: for example; If a man in open court should affirme before the Judge; Such a one fell out with me, and cursed me, giving me threatening words, that I should smart for it, and some mischeife should light upon my person or goods, are it were long. Upon these curses and threats presently such and such evils befell me, and I suffered these and these losses. The magistrate thus informed may safely proceede to inquire into the matter, but he hath not from hence any sure ground of conviction. For it pleaseth God many times to lay his hand upon mens persons and goods, without the procurement of Witches. And yet experience shewed, that ignorant people, who carry a rage against them, will make strong proofes of such presumptions, whereupon sometimes Jurers do give their Verdict against parties innocent. Lastly, if a man beeing dangerously sicke, and like to die, upon suspition will take it on his death, that such a one hath bewitched him, it is an allegatió of the same nature, which may moove the Judge to examine the party, but it is of no moment for conviction. The reason is, because it was but the suspition of one man, and a mans owne word for himselfe, though in time of extremitie, when it is likely he will speake nothing but the truth, is of no more force then another mans word against him. And these are the proofes, which men in place and time have ordinarily used, for the detecting of such ungodly persons: but the best that may be said of them, is that they be all either false or uncertaine signes, or unavailable for the condemnation of any man whatsoever. Now follow the true proofes, and sufficient meanes of conviction, all which may be reduced to two heads. The first, is the free and voluntary confession of the crime, made by the party suspected and accused after examination. This bath been thought generally of all men both Divines, and Lawyers a proofe sufficient. For what needes more witnesse or further inquirie, when a man from the touch of his own conscience acknowledgeth the fault. And yet the patrons and advocates of Witches except against it, and object in this manner; that a man or woman may confesse against themselves an untruth, being urged thereto either by feare or threatening, or by a desire upon some grieve to be out of the world; of at least, being in trouble, and perswaded it is the best course to save their lives, and obtaine liberty, they may upon simplicitie be induced to confesse that which they never did, even against themselves. Ans. I say not that a bare confession is sufficient, but a confession after due examination taken upon pregnant presumptions. For if a man examined, without any ground or presumptions, should openly acknowledge the crime, his act may be justly suspected, as grounded upon by-respects; but when proceeding is made against him at the first, upon good probabilities, and hereupon he be drawn to a free confession, that which be hath manifested thereby, cannot but be a truth. Other points of exception urged by them, are of small moment, and may easily be answered out of the grounds before delivered and therefore I omit them. Now if the party helde in suspition, be examined, and will not confesse, but obstinately persist in deniall, as commonly it falleth out; then there is another course to be taken by a second sufficient means of conviction: which is, the testimony of two witnesses, of good and honest report, avouching before the Magistrate upon their owne knowledge, these two things: Either that the party accused, hath made a league with the devil; or hath done some knowne practises of Witchcraft. And all arguments that do necessarily proove either of these, beeing brought by two sufficient witnesses, are of force fully to convince the party suspected. For example: First, if they can proove that the party suspected, hath invocated and called upon the devil, or desired his helpe. For this is a brách of that worship, which Satan bindeth his instruments to give unto him. And it is a pregnant proofe of a league formerly made between thé. Secondly, if they can give evidence, that the party hath intertaiued a familiar spirit, and had conference with, in forme or likenesse of a mouse, cattle, or some other visible creature. Thirdly, if they affirme upon oath, that the suspected person hath done any action or work, which necessarily inferreth a covenant made; as that he hath shewed the face of a man suspected beeing absent, in a glasse; or used Inchantment, or such like feats. In a word, if they both can avouch upon their owne proper knowledge, that such a man or woman suspected, have put in practise any other actions of Witchcraft, as to have divined of things afore they come to passe, and that peremptorily; to have raised tempests, to have caused the form of a dead man to appeare, or the like, standing either in divination or operation, it prooveth sufficiently that he or she is a Witch. But some may say, if these be the onely strong proofes for the conviction of a Sorcerer, it will be then impossible to put any one to death, because the league with Satan is closely made, and the practises of Sorcery are also very secret, and hardly can a man be brought, which upon his owne knowledge, can averred such things. I answer, howsoever both the ground and practise be secret, and to many, unknowne, yet there is a way to come to the knowledge thereof. For it is visual with Satan to promise any thing, till the league be ratified: but when it is once made, and the party intangled in society with him, then he endeavoureth nothing more, then his or her discovery, and useth all meanes possible to disclose them. So that what end soever the Witch propoundeth to her selfe in the league, he intendeth nothing else, but her utter confusion. Therefore in the inst indgement of God, it often falleth out, that these which are true Witches indeede, shall either by confession discover themselves, or by true testimonie be convinced. The causes which moove the Devil not only to effect, but to hasten this discoverie, are two principally. The first is, his malice to wards all men, in so high a degree, that he cannot indure they should enjoy the world, or the benefits of this life (if it were possible) so much as one houre. Though therefore by vertue of the precontract, he be cock-sure of his instrument, yet his malice is not herewith satisfied, till the party be brought to light, and condemned to death. Which may be a caveat to all ill disposed persons, that they beware of yielding themselves unto him. The second, is his insatiable desire of the present and full possession of them, whom he hath got within the bonds of the covenant. For though he have good hope of them, yet is he not certain of their continuance. The reason is, because some united with him in confederacie, have through the great mercy of God, by carefull usage of holy meanes, and faith in Christ, been reclaimed and delivered out of his bondage, and so at length freed from his covenant, so as the hath eternally left them. Hence it is, that he labours by might and maine, to keepe them in ignorance, and to prevent the usage of meanes effectuall to their conversion, by laying a plot for their discovery. But how then comes it to passe, that all such persons are not speedily detected, but some live long, and others die without any mans privity? Ans. The reasons hereof may be divers. First, because some one or more of them may belong to Gods election: and therefore albeit for causes best knowne to himselfe, he suffer them for a time to be holden in the snares of Satan, yet at length in mercie he reclaimes them, and in the meane time suffereth not the devil to exercise the depth of his malice in discovering them to their confusion. Againe, for others, the Lord may in justice and anger suffer them not to be disclosed, that living under the meanes, where they might be reclaimed, and wilfully contemning the same; they may live to fill up the measure of their iniquities, and thereby be made finally inexcusable, that they may receive their juster condemnation. Secondly, the devil suffereth some to live long undisclosed, that they may exercise the greater measure of his malice in the world; specially if they be parties malitiously bent to doe hurt to men, and other creatures. Thirdly, some Witches do warily agree with the Devil, for a certaine tearme of yeares, during which time he bindeth himselfe not to hurt them, but to be at their command. And Satan is carefull, specially in case of his owne advantage, to keepe touch with them, that they may the more strongly leave unto him on their parts. But if the case so stand, that neither the partie suspected confesseth, nor yet sufficient witnesses can be produced, which are able to convict him or her, either of these two wayes; we have no werrant out of the word either in generall, or in speciall, to put such an one to death. For though presumption bee never so strong, yet they are not proofes sufficient for conviction, but onely for examination. I would therefore wish and advise all Jurers, who give their Verdict upon life and death in courts of Affises, to take good heede, that as they be diligent in zeale of Gods glorie, and the good of his Church, in detecting of Witches, by all sufficient and lawfull means; so likewise they would be carefull what they do, and not to condemne any party suspected upon bare presumptions, without sound and sufficient proofes, that they be not guilty through their owne rashnesse of shedding innocent blood. Sect. III. Quest. III. Whether a man may prevent the danger of Witchcraft, and if he may, then what Remedies he may lawfully and effectually use against it?

To this Question we answer affirmatively, that a man may. And for the manifestation of this point, the Remedies of Witchcraft are to be considered. In the handling whereof, I will proceede in this order. First, to set down the true, lawfull, and effectuall Remedies allowed and prescribed in the word. Secondly, the unlawfull and superstitious means prescribed and practised in the Romish Church. Lawfull Remedies of Witchcraft, be of two sorts; Preservative, and Restorative. Preservative are those, which keepe a man from the hurt of Witchcraft. And these be of two sorts; either such as keepe safe the persons of men, or such as preserve the places of mens aboad. For the Persons of men, there is one soveraigne preservative; And that is, to be within the covenant of grace, made and confirmed in the Gospel by the blood of Christ, and that not outwardly in profession onely, as all those be which are within the compasse of the Church, but truly and indeed as all the Elect are. And a man is then in the covenant, when God of his grace in the use of the meanes, gives him a true knowledge of the nature of it, and of conditions required in the same on both parts: and withall gives him a true and lively faith, to apprehend and apply to himselfe the promise of God in Christ, touching remission of sinnes, and life everlasting: yea further to shew forth his faith by the fruits of true repentance, and new obedience. When a man in this manner comes to be brought within the covenant, and is in Christ, he then receives assurance of Gods favour, and to him belong the promises depending thereupon, to wit, not onely of the comfortable presence of Gods spirit, but of the presence and speciall protection of his holy Angells, to pitch their tents about him, to keepe him safe in soule and body, from the power and malicious practises of Satan, and his members. The ground of this assurance is laid downe in the word, Psal. 92. 10. He shall give his Angels charge over thee, and c. And the speech of Balaam confirmed the same, who when he was hired of Balaa to curse Gods people, and had oftentimes assayed to do it, but could not, at last he breakes out into this confession. There is no Witch-craft against Jacob, nor Sorcerie against Israel: (for so the words are to be read, according to the true meaning, and circumstances of the text.) As if he should have said, I was of thy opinion (O Balac) that Israel might be cursed, but after triall made, I found by good experience, that I could doe that people of God no hurt by mine Inchantments. Howbeit we must here remember, that the promise of protection made unto Gods children, is not absolute, but admitteth exception, as all other promises of temporall blessings do, and that in this manner: Thou shalt be partaker of this or that blessing, and this or that curse shall be remooved, if it be expedient for thee: but if for speciall causes to try thy faith, and to exercise thy patience, I make deniall, thou must rest thy selfe contented in my good will and pleasure. By werrant of this doctrine, a question commonly mooved, may be resolved: Whether the servant and childe of God, may be bewitched or not? Out of that which hath been said, I answer, he may; and that is plaine by the word. For by Gods permission, the holy body of

Christ himselfe was by Satan transported from place to place, Matth.4. Righteous Job was miserably afflicted in his body by the power of the Devil; and his children, who no doubt were Gods servants, and brought up in his feare, as their father was, were slaine by the same power. Yea Christ himselfe testifieth, Luk. 13.16. That a daughter of Abraham, that is, of the faith of Abraham, had beene troubled eighteene yeares with a spirit of insirmitie, which the devil caused by bowing her body together, so as she could not lift her selfe up, v. 11. And therefore whereas some men are of this minde, that their faith is so strong, that all the Witches in the world, and all the devils in hell cannot hurt them; they are much deceived. This their faith is but a fond presumption, and no true faith. For no man in the earth can absolutely assure himselfe of safety and protection from the devil: and if any could, it were the child of God; but Salomon saith, that all outward things may come alike both to the good and to the bad, Eccles. 9.2. Howbeit in this case there is great difference betweene the servant of God, and an unrepentant sinner. Though the godly man be not exempted from Witchcraft, yet he is a thousand folde more free from the power thereof, then other men are. For there is onely one case, and no more, wherein the devil hath any way power to hurt him, and that is, when it pleaseth God by that kind of crosse, to make triall of his saith and patience; and out of this case, he is alwaies free from the annoyance of the vilest Witches in the world. If then this be the onely soveraigne preservative to keepe a man safe and sure from the power of Witches, and of the Devil, to have part in the covenant of grace, to be made partaker of Christ, by a true faith, testified by dying unto all sinne, and living unto God in newnesse of life: we must not content our selves with a formall profession, as many in the visible Church doe, which wanting the life of faith, doe not live in Christ; but strive to go further, and to adorne our profession, by framing our lives according to the word, that we may have our portion in this excellent priviledge of preservation, from the power and malice of the enemies of God, and all ungodly persons. Preservatives of the second sort, are such as concerne the places of mens aboad. For Sathan contenteth not himselfe to have manifested his malice in assisting mens persons, but he also enlargeth the same to the molestation of the places where they dwell, by infecting the ayre, and such like. The onely effectuall means to remedie this evil, is a Sanctification of the places of our habitation. Looke as we are wont to sanctifie our meat and drink, by Gods word and by prayer, and thereby procure his blessing upon his owne ordinance for our refreshing: so in like manner may wee sanctifie the places of our aboad, and thereby both procure the blessing which we want, and also avoide many curses and dangers, which otherwise would fall upon us. If any shall thinke the Consecration of houses and places in this fort, to be a meere devise of mans braine; let them remember, that in the Old Testament, besides the dedication of the Temple, allowed by all, there was a Law prescribed to the Jewes; for the speciall dedication of every mans house: If any man hath built a new house (saith Moses) and hath not dedicate it, let him return again, and c. Deut. 20.5. As who should say, he hath omitted a necessarie dutie. Nowe this dedication was nothing else, but the sanctification of them by word and prayer, wherein they made acknowledgment, that they became theirs by the free gift and blessing of God, and further desired a free and lawful use of the same to his glorie, and their mutuall good. A dutie which hath been performed by the servants of God in ancient times. The first thing that Abraham did, when he came from Vr of the Chaldeans, to the land of Canaan, which God gave him to possesse, was the building of an Altar for the worship of God, his sacrificing thereon, and calling upon the name of the Lord, Gen. 12. 8. The same did Noah before him at his first comming out of the Arke after the flood, Gen. 8. 20, and Jacob after him in Bethel. And they were all mooved herunto, because they knew their comfortable aboad in those places, came not by their owne endeavour, but from the blessing of god. When the good King Hezekiah kept the Pass over in Jerusalem, his principall care was that the priests and all the people might first be sanctified, and therefore he prayed unto God to be mercifull to them that were not sanctified, 2. Chron. 30. 18. And as he behaved him selfe in his kingdom, so should every master of a family behave himselfe in his house where he dwelleth, labouring to sanctifie the same that it may be comfortable to him and his; least for neglect thereof, he pull upon himselfe, and those that belong unto him, the heavy hand of God, in plagues and punishments. The second kind of Remedies are Restorative, which serve to deliver men from Witchcraft, by curing the hurts of Witches in the bodies of men, or other creatures. In the handling where, first, we will consider, how whole countries, and then how every private man may be cured and delivered. Whole Countries, and Kingdoms are freed and cured specially by one meanes; The publishing and embracing of the Gospell. When our Saviour Christ had sent the seaventie Disciples to preach in Jurie; at their returne he gave this testimonie of the effect of their ministerie, That he sawe Satan fall downe from heaven like lightening, Luk. 10. 18. his meaning was this, As lightning is suddenly and violently sent out of the cloud, and (as it were) cast downe to the earth by the cracke of the thunder: even so Satan the Prince of the world that ruleth in the hearts of the disobediet, was cast downe, and his kingdome ruinated by the power of the Gospel preached. In the times of ignorance the devil triumpheth freely without controlement, but the myst and darkenesse of his delusions cannot possibly abide the bright beames of gods glorious will revealed by preaching. The Lord of ancient times commanded his people not to 'doe according to those nations, among whom they dwelt in Canaan, by practising Witchcraft, or following after Sorcerie, Deut. 18. 9. and c. And that they might be able to obey this commandement, Moses prescribeth unto them this restorative, the reverent and obedient hearing of the Lords Prophets, vers. 18. In this our Church if wee would be healed of our wounds, and banish Sathan from among us, who greatly annoyeth a great number of our people by his delusions and damnable practises of Sorcerie: the onely way to bring it to passe, is the maintaining of a learned Ministerie, the advancing of Propl. ets, by whose labours the Gospell may flourish. For the faithfull dispensation thereof is the Lords owne arme and scepter, whereby he beateth downe the kingdome of darkenesse, and confoundeth the devil and enterprises of the devil. The second fort of Restoratives, serves for the cure of particular persons: for howsoever the gift and power of casting out of devils, and curing witchcraft be ordinarily ceased, since the Apostles times, it being a gift peculiar to the Primitive Church, and given to it only during the infancie of the Gospell; yet there may be means used and that effectual, for the easing of any person that is bewitched by Satans instruments. Those therefore that are in these daies tormented in this kind, must doe three things. First, they must enter into serious examination of themselves, and consider the cause for which it pleaseth God to suffer Satan to exercise the with that kind of crosse. And here upon diligent inquirie, they shall find that their owne sinnes are the true and proper causes of these evils. When Saul was disobedient to the commandement of God, the Lord sent upon him an evil spirit to vexe him, 1. Sam. 15. Hymeneus and Alexander for their pestilent errors were both cast out of the Church, and given up also to Satan, that they might learne not to blaspheme, 2. Tim. 1. 20. in the same manner was the incestuous person dealt withall, 1. Cor. 5. 5.

Secondly, after this Examination, the same parties must shewe forth their faith, whereby they depend on the free favour and mercie of God for their deliverance. How may this be done? by hearty prayer unto God, joyned with fasting, that the same may be more earnest. In which praier the maine desire of the heart must be absolutely for the pardon of their sins, and then for deliverance from the hurts and torments of diabolical persons: yet not absolutely as for the other, but with this condition, so far forth as it stands with Gods glorie, and their owne good. For these are the bounds and limits of all temporall good things; of them the Lord maks no absolute promise, but with these conditions and qualifications. Thirdly, the parties bewitched must patiently beare the present annoyance, comforting themselves with this, that it is the Lords owne hand, by whose speciall providence it comes to passe, and who turneth al things to the good of his chosen. Againe, they are to remember, that he beeing a most wise God, and loving Father in Christ, will not suffer them to be tried about that they are able to beare, but in his good time will grant a joyful issue. Now when the bewitched shall thus submit themselves unto God, in the crosse be it that he (upon some causes) defer their deliverance, yet they shall not finally be deceived of their hope. For either in this life, at the appointed time, or in the end of this life, by death they shall be eternally delivered, and put in present possession of everlasting ease and happinesse. Thus much of the true Remedies against Witchcraft. In the next place we are a little to examine the false and superstitious Remedies, prescribed and used by them of the Popish Church. The most learned Papists of this age doe teach and avouch, that there is in Gods church an ordinary gift and power, whereby some men may cast out devils, and helpe annoyances that come by Witches. The Protestant is of a contrarie judgement, and holdeth according to truth, that there is now no such ordinary gift left to the Church of God, since the daies of the Apostles. Reasons of this opinion may be these. First, casting out of devils, and curing such annoyances, are extraordinary and miraculous works. For Christ accounteth handling of serpents without hurt, speaking with new tógues, curing of diseases by imposition of hands, (all which are things of lesse moment) to be miracles, Mark, 16. 18. 19. but all these lesser works, yea the ordinarie power of working them, is ceased: for it was onely given to the Apostles in the Primitive Church, as a meanes to confirme the doctrine of the Gospel to unbelievers that never heard of Christ before. So Paul faith, Strange tongues (that is, the gift of speaking strange languages, without ordinary teaching) are for a signe, not to them that believe, but to them that believe not, 1. Cor. 14. 22. And for the same end were all extraordinary gifts then given. Seeing therefore the doctrine of the Gospell hath been already established, and the truth thereof sufficiently confirmed by miracles in the Primitive Church, the same gift must needs cease unto us. For if it should still continue, it would call into question the effect of the Apostolicall preaching, and implie thus much, that the Gospel was not well established, nor sufficiently confirmed by their extraordinary Ministery, and miracles accompanying the same. Againe, if the gift of working miracles should remaine, then the promise of God for his speciall and extraordinary assistance therein should yet continue; for the gift and promise goe together; so long as the promise is in force, so long is the gist also; but the promise made by Christ, In my name shall they cast out devils, and speake with newe tongues, Mark. 16. was in force onely in the persons and Ministery of the Apostles, and those that had extraordinarie and immediate calling from God; and it ceased when they and their calling ceased. Therefore if Ministers now should lay their hands on the sicke, they should not recover them: if they should annoint them with oyle, it should do them no good, because they have no promise. Howbeit the Papists stand stiffely in defending the continuance of these gifts. First, they say, the Church of the Newe Testaments is nothing inferiour to that of the Old. The Jewish Church before the comming of Christ, was the Church of the Old. Testament, and had the power and gift of casting out Devils. So saith our Saviour himselfe, Marth. 12. 27. If I through Beelzebub cast out devils, then by whome doe your children cast them out? In which words hee ascribeth this gift unto the Jewes, therefore it should seeme, that the same remaineth still in the Church. Anf. That place of Scripture is diversly expounded: Some by children there mentioned, understand the Apostles, who were Jewes borne, and had received from Christ this gift and power to cast out devils. Which if it be so, it maketh not for them, because they had it extraordinarily.

But I rather thinke, that by children, are meant the Exorcising Jewes, before Christs time, who did cast out devils amóg the, pretending an abilitie to doe this worke in the name of God; whereas in truth, they were all flat Sorcerers, and did it by vertue of a league and compact made with the devil. Which practise hath been of long continuance, and is at this day common and usual among the Popish sort. And that there were such Exorcists among the Jewes, it is evident. For such were those Vagabonds which came to Ephesus, and tooke upon them to cast out devils by the name of Jesus, and Paul, Act. 19. 13. but the man in whome the euill spirit was, (so soone as he had adjured the spirit) ranne upon them, and mightily prevailed against them, vers. 16. Now if they had done this great worke by the power of God (as they pretended) the holy Ghost would not have called them Exorcists and Vagabonds, neither could the evil spirit possibly have overcome them as he did. Againe, in the Historie of the Jewes are recorded many practises of such as exercise this power among them. Raphael the Angell telleth Tobias, that a perfume made of the heart and liver of a fish, will helpe a man vexed with an evil spirit, Tob.6. 7. which counsell is flat Magick, for there is no such vertue in the liver of a fish. And in other histories we reade, that one Eleazar a Jew, by the smell of a certain roote put to the nose of a man possessed with a devil, caused the devil to come out of his nosthrills, and forsake him; which thing was done in publike place before Vespasian and others. This also was effected by meere conjuration. For what vertue can there be in any roote or hearb in the world, availeable to command and enforce Satan to depart from a man possessed? And yet such feats were plaied by sundry Magicians among the Jewes. Wherupon I conclude, that the meaning of our Savior in the place alledged, is in effect thus much: If I by the power of Beelzebub, and c. that is, you have among you sundry Magicians and Exorcists, who pretend and Exercise the gift of casting out devils, and you thinke they doe it by the power of God, why then do you not carie the same opinion of me also? The second reason, is grounded on the promise of Christ, Mark. 16. 17. These tokens shall follow them that believe, In my name they shall cast out devils, and c. whence they gather, that there shall be alwaies some in the Church, who shall have power to cast forth devils, if they believe. Ans. That promise was made by Christ unto his Church, to be fulfilled immediately after his ascension. It did not extend to all times, and persons, so long as the world endureth, but only to the times of the primitive Church, and to such as then lived, For to them only the doctrin of the Gospell was to be confirmed by signes and miracles. And this lasted about 200, yeares next after Christ his ascension. During which time, not onely the Apostles and Ministers, but even private men, and souldiers wrought many miracles. The third reason is taken from experience, which (as they say) in al ages from the Apostles times to this day sheweth, that there have bin alwaies some in the Church, which have had this gift of casting out Devils, and curing the hurts of Witchcraft. Ans. This gift continued not much above the space of 200, years after Christ. From which time many heresies beganne to spread themselves; and then shortly after Popery that mysterie of iniquitie beginning to spring up, and to dilate it selfe in the Churches of Europe, the true gift of working Miracles then ceased; and in stead thereof came in delusions, and lying wonders, by the effectuall working of Satan, as it was foretold by the Apostle, 2. Thels.2.9. Of which sort were and are all those miracles of the Romish Church, whereby simple people hath beene notoriously deluded. These indeed have there continued from that time to this day. But this gift of the holy Ghost, where of Question is made, ceased long before. To proceed yet further, we are here to consider the particular Remedies which they of the Popish Church have prescribed against the hurts that have come by Witchcraft. And they are principally five. I. The name Jesus. II. The use of the Reliques of Saints. III. The singe of the Crosse. IV. Hallowed creatures. V. Exorcismes. I. First, for the name Jesus: Thus much we grant, that any Christian may lawfully call upon the name of Jesus in prayer, for the helpe and deliverance of these that are possessed and bewitched, but yet with the caveat and condition before specied, If it be the will of God, and if their recoverie may make for his glory, the benefit of the Church, and the good of the parties diseased. But the Papist by the use of this name, intendeth a further matter, to wit, that the very name uttered in so many letters and sillables, is powerfull to cast out Devils, and to helpe those that are bewitched. For when it is uttered, then (say they) the authoritie of Christ is present, that the worke may be done. A flat untruth, and a practise full of danger. For let this be well considered, whatsoever any man doth in this case; he must doe it by vertue of his calling, and have also his warrant for the doing there of out of the word; which if he want, and yet will undertake such a worke, he may justly feare the like event that befell the vagabond Jewes that were Exorcists, Act. 19. 13. Now the Church of Christ hath no warrant in the word, to use this name of Christ for any such purpose; neither hath any ordinarie Christian a speciall calling from God so to doe. Therefore he may not doe it. And whereas they would beare men in hand, that the said name, of all the names of Christ, and above all other things, is of most speciall vertue, though it be used even by a man that wanteth faith, because the Apostle saith, At the name of Jesus every knee shall bowe, bath of things in heaven, in earth, and under the earth, Phil. 2. 10. and by things under the earth are meant the devils: we must know that their allegation is weake, and that they greatly abuse the place. For there the name Jesus, is not onely a title of Christ, but withall signifieth the power, majeftie, and authoritie of Christ, sitting at the right had of the father, to which all creatures in heaven, earth, and hell are made subject; and by that power indeed (if they had it at commaund) they might be able to cure the hurts of Witchcraft.

II. The second speciall Remedie is the Use of Saints Reliques; as their books, bones, apparell, staves, or such like, which beeing but touched of the parties vexed, are excellent meanes to recover them. Ans: The use of these things, to the purposes aforesaid, is a meere superstitious practise. For first, they have not the true Reliques of the Saints, as would plainely appeare, if a true Inventorie were taken of al such as they say are to be found in their Monasteries and Churches. Secondly, though they had them, yet have they no warrant or calling to use them to this ende: for in all the word of God, there is neither commandemet to warrant the use, nor promise to assure any man of a blessing upon the use of them. Albeit they would seeme to have some warrant, and therefore they alleadge that which is written, 2. King 13. 21. of a dead man, who beeing for hast throwne into the sepulchre of Elisha, so soone as he touched the bones of Elisha, revived, and stood upon his feete. To this also they adde the examples of cures done by Peters shadowe, Act. 5. 15. and sundry diseases healed by Pauls handkerchifes, Act. 19. 12. Ans. These things indeede are true, but they serve nothing to their purpose. For first, the quickening of the dead souldier, came not from any vertue in the corps of Elisha; but it was a miracle, which it pleased God then to worke, by meanes of the corps, that the Jewes at that time might be confirmed in the truth of that doctrine, which Elisha had taught them from God, and which before his death they had neglected, as I have before shewed. And it was a thing only then done, and never since. It cannot therefore be a ground for the ordinary use of Reliques. Againe, touching the other examples: I answer, that both Peter and Paul had the gift of working Miracles, and having the gift, they might use such meanes for the present to cure diseases. But the Papists are not able to shewe, that God hath given them the like gift, whereby they might be warranted for the use of the like meanes: neither can they assuredly hope for successe, although they should undertake to use them. III. The third Remedie, is the signe of the Crosse, made upon the body of the party tormented. Behold to what a height of impietie they are grown ascribing that to the creature, which is proper to the Creator. For the power of working miracles, is proper onely to the Godhead. The Prophets and Apostles in their times did not worke them of themselves, but were onely Gods passive instruments, in this manner: When the Lord intended by them to worke any miracle, they received from him at the same time an extraordinary and speciall instinct, whereby they were mooned to attempt the worke. They therefore yielded themselves to the prefer motion of Gods spirit, to be his instruments onely in the dispensation of the worke: but the sole author and producer of the miracle, was God himselfe. And in this case the very manhood of our Saviour Christ, considered apart from his Godhead, had no power of it selfe, but was onely the instrument of his Godhead, whensoever it pleased him in that kind to manifest the same. Wherefore to ascribe this vertue to the Crosse, beeing a creature, or the worke of a creature, is to communicate the incommunicable power of the Creator to it, which is plaine blasphemie. IV. The fourth Remedie, is the using of hallowed things; as hallowed graines, salt, water, bread, images; specially the image of Agnus dei. Ans. Hallowed creatures are in truth unhallowed superstitions. For every creature is sanctified by the word and praier, 1. Tim.4.4. by the word, when God in his word commands us to use it for some end; and by prayer, when we give him thankes for giving the creature, and withall desire his blessing in the use thereof. Now let any Papist shew me one letter or sillable in all the Booke of God, commanding the use of a creature for any such ende. They affirme indeede, that Elisha wrought miracles by hallowed salt, for by it he cured the bitter waters, 2.King.2. 21. But the Prophet used not hallowed, but common salt, and that not ordinarily, but onely then, as a meanes whereby to worke a miracle. It was therefore powerfull in his hands, because for the doing thereof, he had power and warrant from God extraordinarily: and it cannot be so in any other, which hath not the same gift. V. The fift and last Remedie, is Exorcisme, which is an adjuring and commanding the Devil in the name of God, to depart fró the party possessed, and cease to molest him any more. This meanes was used by our Savior Christ himselfe, and after him by his Apostles, and other belevers in the time of the Primitive Church, when the gift of working Miracles was in force: but in these daies (as I said before) that gift is ceased, and also the promise of power annexed to the use of adjuration: and therefore the meanes thereof must needs cease. And for an ordinary man now to command the Devil in such sort, is meere presumption, and a practise of Sorcerie. Sect. IV. IV. Quest. Whether the Witches of our age are to be punished with death, and that by vertue of this law of Moses? I doubt not, but in this last age of the world, among us also, this sin of Witchcraft ought as sharply to be punished as in the former times; and all Witches being throughly convicted by the Magistrate, ought according to the Law of Moses to be put to death. For proofe hereof, consider these teasons. First, this Law of Moses flatly enjoyneth all men, in all ages, without limitation of circumstances, not to suffer the Witch to live; and hereupon I gather, that it must stand the same both now and for ever to the worlds end. Patrons of Witches except against this, holding that it was a Judiciall Lawe which continued but for a time, and concerned onely the Nation of the Jewes, and is now ceased. But I take the contrary to be the truth, and that upon these grounds. I. Those Judiciall Lawes, whose penalty is death, because they have in them a perpetuall equitie, and doe serve to maintaine some moral precept, are perpetuall. The Jewes indeed had some Lawes of this kind, whose punishments were temporall, and they lasted onely for a certaine time; but the penaltie of Witchcraft, beeing Death by Gods appointment, and the inflicting of that punishment serving to maintain the equitie of the three first morall precepts of the first Table, which cannot be kept unless this Lawe be put in execution; it must necessarily follow, that it is in that regard morall, and binds us, and shall in like sort bind all men in all ages, as well as the Jewes themselues, to whom it was at that time personally directed. II. Every Judiciall Law, that hath in it the equitie of the Law

129

of nature, is perpetuall; but this Law of punishing the Witch by death, is such. For it is a principle of the Law of nature, holden for a grounded truth in all Countries and Kingdoms, among all people in every age; that the traytor who is an enemie to the State, and rebelleth against his lawfull Prince, should be put to death; now the most notorious traytor and rebell that can be, is the Witch. For she renounceth God himselfe, the King of Kings, shee leaves the societie of his Church and people, she bindeth her selfe in league with the devil: and therefore if any offender among men, ought to suffer death for his fact, much more ought shee, and that of due desert. The second reason for the proofe of the point in hand is this: According to Moses law, every Idolater was to be stoned to death: Deut. 17. ver. 3,4,5. If there be found any among you, that hath gone and served other gods, as the Sunne, the Moone, or any of the hoast of heaven: if the thing upon enquirie be found to bee true and certaine, thou shalt bring them forth unto thy gates, whether it be man or woman, and shalt stone them with stones till they die. Now this is the very case of a Witch, she renounceth the true God, and maketh choice to serve the devil, she is therefore a grosse Idolater, and her punishment must be sutable. It is alleadged by the favourers of the contrarie part, that Peter denied Christ, and yet was not put to death: I answer, there is great difference betweene Peters denyall of Christ, and Witches denying of God. Peters deniall was upon infirmitie and in hast: the Witch denieth God upon knowledge and deliberation, wittingly and willingly. Againe, Peter did not upon his deniall betake himselfe to the Devil, but turned unto Christ again, which he testified by his heartie and speedie repentance: but witches deny God, and betake themselves to the devil, of their owne accord, as is manifest even by their own confessions, at their arraignments. The third reason. Everie seducer in the Church, whose practise was to draw men from the true God to the worship of Idols, though it were a mans owne sonne or daughter, wife or friend, by the peremptorie decree and commandment of God, was at no hand to be spared or pitied, but the hand of the witnesse first, and then the hands of all the people must bee upon him, to kill him, Deut. 13.6.9. If this be so, no Witches convicted ought to escape the sword of the Magistrate; for they are the most notorious seducers of all others. When they be once intangled with the Devils league, they labour to inure their dearest friends and posterity, in their cursed and abominable practises: that they may bee the more easily drawne into the same confederacie, wherewith they themselves are united unto Sathan. I might here alleadge, that they deserve death because many of them be murtherers, but I stand not upon that instance, because I hold in the general that Witches are not to be suffered to lieu, though they doe no hurt either to man or other creatures, and that by vertue of Moses lawe, onely for their leagues sake, whereby they become rebels to God, Idolaters and seducers, as now hath been shewed. Yet not with standing all that hath been said, many things are brought in defense of them, by such as be their friends and welwillers. First, it is said, that the hurt that is done, comes not from the Witch, but from the devil; he deserves the blame because it is his worke, and she is not to die for his sinne. Answ. Let it be granted, that the Witch is not the author of the evil that is done, yet she is a confederate and partner with the devil in the fact, and so the lawe takes hold on her. See it in a familiar comparison. A company of men conspire together in a robbery, by common consent some stand in open place to espie out the bootie, and to give the watch-word, others are set about the passage, privily to rush upon the man, and to spoyle him of his goods. In this case what saith the law? The Parties that gave the watchword, though they did nothing to the man, yet beeing accessories and abettors to the robbery by consent, they are theeues, and liable to condemnation and execution, as well as the principalls. Even so stands the case with the Witch. In the working of wonders, and in all mischeivous practises, he or shee is partaker with the devil by consent of covenant: the Witch onely useth the watchword in some charme or otherwise, and doth no more; the devil upon notice given by the Charme, takes his opportunities, and works the mischief. He is the principall agent, but the other yieldeth help, and is rightly liable to punishment. The reason is, because if the devil were not stirred up, and provoked by the Witch, he would never do so much hurt as he doth. He had never appeared in Samuels likenes had he not been sollicited by the Witch of Endor. He would not have caused counterfeit serpents and frogges to appeare in Egypt, but for Jannes and Jambres, and other Inchanters. And in this age there would not in likelihood be so much hurt and hindrance procured unto men, and other creatures by his meanes, but for the instigation of ill disposed persons, that have fellowship and societie with him. Againe, they object, that Witches convicted either repent, or repent not: If they repent, then God pardoneth their sinne, and why should not the Magistrate as well save their bodies, and let them live, as God doth their soules. If they do not repent, then it is a dangerous thing for the Magistrate to put them to death: for by this meanes he kills the bodie, and casts the soule to hell. Answ. All Witches judicially and lawfully convicted, ought to have space of repentance granted unto them, wherein they may be instructed and exhorted, and then afterward executed. For it is possible for them to be saved by Gods mercie, though they have denied him. Secondly, the Magistrate must execute justice upon malefactors lawfully convicted, whether they repent or not. For God approoveth the just execution of judgment upon men without respect to their repentance: neither must their impenitencie hinder the execution of Justice. When the people of Israel had committed Idolatrie in worshipping the golden calfe, Moses did not expect their repentance, and in the meane while forbeare the punishment, but he and the Levites presently tooke their swords, and slew them, and the Lord approved their course of proceeding, Exod.32.28. When Zimri an Israelite had committed fornication with Cozbi a Midianitish woman, Phineas in zeale of Gods glorie, executed judgement on the both, without any respect unto their repentáce, Numb.25.8. and is therefore commended, Psa. 106. 30. Warres are a worthy ordinance of God, and yet no Prince could ever attempt the same lawfully, if every souldier in the field should stay the killing of his enemie, upon expectation of his repentance. And whereas they say, that by executing an impenitent Witch, the Magistrate casteth away the soule; we must know, that the end of execution by the Magistrate is not the damnation of the malefactors soule, but that fin may be punished that others may beware of the like crimes and offences, and that the wicked might be taken away from among Gods people. But some Witches there be that cannot bee convicted of killing any: what shall become of them? Ans. As the killing Witch must die by another law, though he were no Witch; so the healing and harmelesse Witch must die by this Law, though he kill not, onely for covenant made with Sathan. For this must alwaies be remembred as a conclusion, that by Witches we understand not those onely which kill and torment; but all Diviners, Charmers, Juglers, all Wizzards commonly called wise men and wise women; yea, whosoever doe any thing (knowing what they do) which cannot be effected by nature or art; and in the same number we reckon all good Witches, which do no hurt but good, which do not spoile and destroy, but save and deliver. All these come under this sentence of Moses, because they deny God, and are confederates with Sathan. By the lawes of England the theise is executed for stealing, and we thinke it just and profitable; but it were a thousand times better for the land, if all witches, but especially the blessing Witch might suffer death. For the theise by his stealing, and the hurtfull Inchanter by charming, bring hinderance and hurt to the bodies and goods of men; but these are the right hand of the Devil, by which he taketh and destroyeth the soules of men. Men doe most commonly hate and spitte at the damnifying Sorcerer, as unworthy to live among them; whereas the other is so deare unto them, that they hold themselves and their country blessed, that have him among them; they flie unto him in necessitie, they

133

depend upon him as their God, and by this meanes thousands are carried away to their finall confusion. Death therefore is the just and deserved portion of the good Witch.

FINIS.